Memoirs of
A WINNIPEG
CAB DRIVER

E. EDDY PROULX

Tellwell Talent
www.tellwell.ca

ISBN
978-0-2288-3603-2 (Paperback)

Front cover Acknowledgement

I would like to thank Ziv Gil Kazenstein for the wonderful artwork design on the front cover.

Dedication

This book is dedicated to the people in my life whose spirit and influence have inspired and motivated me in writing this book. They have served as a guide for me in completing this work. First and foremost, my primary inspiration is my beautiful and gorgeous wife with whom I have recently celebrated my 50th wedding anniversary, July 18th Patricia (Marceniuk) my Elmwood girl: My favorite oldest son, Jason Proulx, a resident of Keswick, Ontario: My favorite youngest son, Shayne Proulx, the family imp and tease, a resident of Winnipeg. My favorite daughter, Sarah (Pilon) my favorite brat, and there are more! Brats that is, read on. There's my favorite oldest grandson and best bud, Ryan Pilon. My favorite oldest granddaughter and second best brat, Jordan Pilon, her sibling, my favorite brat in training, Skyra Pilon. Then there is my favorite younger grandson, the ball of energy, Liam Pilon, the sports athlete, then there is Eden Pilon, the tooter and highly intelligent imp of the family, and I cannot forget my favorite the youngest granddaughter, Hazel Pilon, who is my angelic cherub because of her kindhearted and generous nature. I cannot forget my also favorite grandson Alex Proulx, (Radimyer or Radi for short), thanks to the fabrication and trickery when a son was born to my impish son, Shayne, whom I love anyway. As a father in law I certainly need to thank God for blessing me with my favorite son in law, Travis Pilon, a military man and the true hero of our entire family; and finally to my favorite and beautiful Daughter in Law, Andrea Bergman, the dedicated environmentalist, of Winnipeg. As you can see, there are a lot of favorites, and brats, in my family that bring radiant sunshine into my life, on a daily basis. God has been good to me and to all our family. Naturally, all our thanks go out to Him, above all.

Table of Contents

In The Beginning.. I

Welcome to Winnipeg... 5

Welcome to Red PATCH Taxi 7

Chuck.. 8

The Dispatchers 20

Car Versus Taxi 30

Keystone Drunks 34

Creative Crooks 36

Smooth Operator! 39

.08 Aftermath 42

Cowboy Kojack 44

Ghoulish Discovery 47

Way Off Base 50

Spiritual Child.. 52

BEER ANYONE? 55

Red Patch Moving Company............................ 58

Red Patch Mario.. 60

Midnight Laundry 64

Backseat Battles.. 67

Poison Darts! 233

Cheater's Remorse.. 238

Fighting Warriors.. 241

The Christmas Present 243

Coca Cola Avenger 248

Foiled Escape 251

Solo Holliday..253

Rude Store Owner 256

Closing Time 259

Grand Theft Taxi 262

Rainy Days and Mondays....................................264

Taxi Durability 269

In Hot Persuit 271

Mystery Man Fatality 273

Cop or Mass Murderer?..................................... 275

Self Incriminating Witness 279

Restless Runaway...284

The Cretin Of Point Douglas.............................288

Red Patch Weasel 292

Temptation...296

Long Distance teen Tramp Learns Con 300

Meter Phobia... 303

Moving On Out.. 305

Ingrates: Part and Parcel of the Job....................307

Wisecracker... 310

Gnome Fights Back 312

Honesty Feels Good 317

In Need of Rescue 319

Weeping and Wailing and Gnashing of Teeth 321

All in the Family 323

Turn the Tables 325

7-11 Flunkie 327

Wagon Girl 329

Boxed In 332

First to Come, First to Go 336

Personal Weapon Pays Off 338

Roughneck Driver 342

Pick a Lane! 348

Shoulda Ducked! 350

Cops versus Thugs 353

Misplaced Loyalty 356

Deadly Chase 359

Rough Policing 361

A Mother's Pain 365

Cops Cool Wild Rider 368

A word on Uber 370

About the Author 375

Attention Readers 377

In The Beginning

*W*hy write a book called *Memoires of a Winnipeg Cab Driver*? And, how could I expect anyone, anywhere else in the world, to identify with the experiences that I have experienced almost daily? It doesn't matter if you never drove a cab in your life; you surely rode in one on occasion? Some people say that being a bar tender is very much like being a cab driver. Ha! Not even close! I admit serving alcohol to drunks can make you feel like a therapist, especially when they seem to hang on to your every word. But that's where you can draw the line. When serving drinks to drunks the bar tender knows he's going to get paid and is unlikely to be assaulted, no matter how rowdy or drunk a patron may become. On the other hand, a taxi driver never knows if their fare is going to pay, skip out on, rob, assault or murder them. Cab drivers often find themselves facing a myriad of circumstances, situations, and experiences, in their daily interactions with the taxi riding public. Career taxi drivers gain a unique education in humanity. On an average day, a taxi driver may meet between 50 to 100 people from every walk of life imaginable. Because of this wide exposure to a kaleidoscope of people, cabbies tend to morph into and develop that unique personality that defines a taxi driver. For the vast period of time I drove cab, I mostly worked nights. Let me quantify the meaning of that. Remember that dog food commercial on TV where a man in a park throws a Frisbee for his dog to chase. The dog takes off like a shot after it looking vibrant and energetic. Then you hear the announcer's voice say, "That's my dog Rex and he's 12 years old. That's 88 years in people years!" To put this in human perspective I say, "Hi, my name is Emile Proulx and I drive taxi for Red Patch Taxi. I am 35 years old and almost all of my time driving for Red Patch was done on the night shift. That's 120 years in day shift years. I used to tell people that night drivers are kept chained up in the dark at the end of our garage and when it's time for them to work our boss unlocks their chains and lets them loose to work the streets.

This just might explain why cabbies morph into that peculiar cabbie persona that all seasoned taxi drivers worldwide seem to exhibit. You know the ones I'm talking about; the guy with a perpetual toothpick sticking out of the corner of his mouth. The guy or gal with the flippant personality. The career taxi driver, the guy who knows everything you tell him but believes none of it. I'm talking about that guy with a smart ass answer for everything. He's cynical, doubts everything you say and has an answer for everything. He's a wise crack expert. He's been around the block more times than the local transit driver. He or she has seen it all and, somehow, through osmosis, it has becomes interwoven into the very fabric of their character. Nothing can surprise them and even when he or she gets beat for a fare, they always come up with a hilarious line to encapsulate the event. This is universal among all cab drivers, everywhere. So, it doesn't matter if you drove a cab in New York City, Memphis, Chicago, France, London, Vancouver, Lisbon, Bangkok, Toledo, Toronto, Calgary, Dallas, Freeport, Hollywood, Mexico City, Calgary, Hawaii............you get the idea. This book is for you, even if, all you ever did, was live in anyone of those places listed above. This book is about people, maybe even you. We are all woven into the fabric of mankind, yes, into the very culture in which we exist and function. I promise that if you read this book you will see yourself or someone you know, on some of its pages. God bless you for doing so. Read on and enjoy!

Never in my wildest dreams did I ever imagine that one day I would graduate from high school, move to Winnipeg, then become a career taxi driver. If you would have prophesied that to me when I was a teenage, I would have cried like a baby. Then I would have tried my hand at Russian roulette. A taxi driver! Me! No way! I'd rather be a goalie for a dart team! I saw myself in a more hallowed role, such as a police officer or a fireman. Anything but a cab driver! I thought that only a complete failure with a very low I.Q. and no intellect would drive a taxi for a living. Where was the challenge, I thought! I was my own worst critic. I was a high school graduate for Pete sakes! In those days most students ended their education in grade 9 or 10. Very few actually graduated from grade 12 or 13, when there was a grade 13. I was the he first member of my entire family to do so. Everyone told me I had the world by the tail and I was destined for greatness. For the longest time, I was ashamed to tell anyone that I drove cab for a living, especially my family and friends back home, in Kirkland Lake, Ontario, some twelve hundred miles East of Winnipeg. This fact brought me comfort as I felt that I didn't have to worry about running into old school mates, who would undoubtedly grill me about what career I had gotten into. This scenario kept me awake some nights.

Leaving Home: In 1968, I left Kirkland Lake to find my worldly fortune and fame. I boarded the train in the tiny hamlet of Swastika, a distance of approximately 5 miles south west of Kirkland Lake. The train ride was brutal. We left Friday evening around 7 p.m. and arrived Monday morning around 11 a.m. The ride ended when the conductor announced that it was minus 28 degrees below zero Fahrenheit. Like I said earlier, I was a hick from the sticks and had never gone anywhere outside of Kirkland Lake. I was expecting to see huge skyscrapers and office towers but there was none of that.

Welcome to Winnipeg

I started to panic. When 1 arrived at Portage and Main, 1 concluded that this must be the suburbs. When the conductor saw that 1 wasn't preparing myself to exit, he asked me where 1 was going. "Aren't you getting off here,? He asked. "No." 1 answered, "I'm going to Winnipeg."

"This *is* Winnipeg,!" he answered gruffly. My heart sank when 1 looked out the train window as we inched our way along Main Street, toward the main CN depot. The scene was depressing. Thick smoke rose lazily from the chimneys above the antique buildings and 1 could feel the frigid temperatures penetrate me from outside. The Nutty Club business was the tallest buildings 1 could see, and that was only 5 stories high. Eaton's had 8 floors but 1 could not see it from where 1 sat. When 1 told my dad that 1 had decided to go to Winnipeg, he became angry with me. He yelled at me and said it was a stupid idea and that if 1 went to Winnipeg, 1 would be lucky to land a job, shoveling grain for 75 cents an hour! When 1 viewed the frigid scene outside my passenger window, I concluded that I wouldn't be so lucky as to land such a good job. When I finally stepped out through the front doors of the CN Depot, I caught an overwhelming odor of diesel fuel. I decided that I would stay here only until spring before moving on to Vancouver. Anywhere but here had to be better! My first job in Winnipeg saw me employed with Canadian National Railway, certainly a more prestigious titled employer. I was a hostler's helper. My job was to service and help deliver diesel locomotives from the Symington Diesel Shop to other locations throughout the city. Once there, the crew of engineers took possession of them. Then they would hook up to a waiting train and leave for places unknown to me. Later the hostler and I went for lunch in the cafeteria in the C.N. Depot. After we had our meal we took a taxi back to resume our shifts. It was during one of those taxi rides back to the diesel shop that I became intrigued with the world of taxis. I was taken in by the smooth flow of communications between driver and the dispatcher as things moved along without confusion. It intrigued me enough that I eventually, ventured to get my taxi license and began working on a part time basis.

Welcome to Red PATCH Taxi

*I*nitially, it was my intent to moonlight as a taxi driver and earn extra cash. In time, I learned to love the job, mostly because of the people. I became fascinated by the people and their interesting stories. More than anything else, I loved the freedom. I could work any time I felt like it. I could work as many hours as I wanted, or as little hours as I wanted. I could take any and as many days off as I wanted, and no one said boo. I could take weeks off at a time if I wanted, that was okay too. In other words, I had complete control of my life. Any time I showed up for work they were glad I was there. Never in all my years of driving cab did management ream me out for being late or for missing a day's work. They were simply happy whenever I showed up and it made me feel appreciated. On top of all that, I met a lot of wonderful and fascinating people. It was easy for me to transition from part time to full time.

Chuck

*T*he owner of Red Patch Taxi in Winnipeg in the 1970's was a man whom I will simply call Chuck. He was tougher than nails and he ruled his business with an iron fist. The best physical description I can give of him is to compare him to the heavyweight fighting champion of the N.H.L., John Fergusson, who once played for the Montreal Canadians. In comparison to John Fergusson, Chuck was older but was just as tough but meaner. He was in his mid fifties and built like a cement mixer. As tough as he was Chuck was a fair and honest man but God help you if you crossed him.

I was told he started with one car and worked feverishly to build his business. He would work until he couldn't stay awake anymore and slept in his car until he woke up and started work again. He kept building his taxi business until he had amassed 33 cars. He serviced the east side of the city plus a lot of the downtown area. He also covered a good chunk of the north end. Chuck was a World War 2 veteran and he brought a number of fellow fighters with him from the service. Chuck was also in the cattle business and he often made huge sale transactions with the local slaughter houses like Maple Leaf Mills. He treated people with fairness until they did something to him to cause him financial loss and many rumors did float around the office that exaggerated his colorful reputation. Working this hard to build his business made him need to protect his investment which he did fervently.

Chuck usually got into the office about 4 o'clock in morning and boomed about like a bear with a sore ass. You could hear him cursing and screaming his displeasure when dealing with office business issues. His booming voice rattled the windows as he reprimanded the drivers for whatever infractions they may have committed. The worst infraction or sore point for Chuck was car accidents. This subject really sent him off the deep end! The rumor about drivers who got involved in accidents went something like this. It was told that if you got into an accident with one of his taxies, Chuck would take you out in the garage for a pep talk. He would take you to the mangled car in the shop and with his booming voice say to you, "See the cab you destroyed? That car will be sitting in this garage doing nothing for a whole week, which means, I'll be losing money every day, until its back on the road. Besides that, I have to pay people to work on it until it's repaired and I have to buy expensive parts. On top of all that, my insurance costs will climb even higher than what it is now! Your incompetence is costing me a lot of money. We can train monkeys to drive cars but we can't train you to drive. Do you know why?" Without waiting for an answer he would roar, "Because monkeys are smarter than you!" With his voice reaching an explosive pitch, he would violently grab the pathetic driver by the scruff of the neck, bring him up close so that they were nose to nose, and say, "You cost me money, now I'm going to cost you money!" He would then proceed to beat the hapless driver to a pulp. This always meant an ambulance trip to the hospital where the driver usually spent at least a week re-cooperating. The same amount of time it took for the repairs to the smashed up car to occur. I have to admit I have never witnessed such a beating but I have heard such stories so many times, from so many drivers over the years, that I am convinced that they were true. I have often witnessed Chuck stomping through the office yelling at cabbies, destroying property that I view these stories or rumors as corroborating evidence. The rumors were more fact than fiction.

Like I said Chuck was tougher than nails and meaner than a junk yard dog. He wasn't married at the time which was not surprising to anyone, heck, only Calamity Jane or Attila the Hun would have made him a proper wife. Sometimes, a rookie driver would announce to the dispatcher that a fare had skipped out of his car. At times, when Chuck happened to be around, he would meet the driver at the location and the exchange went something like this.

Chuck to rookie: "What happened kid?"

Rookie Driver: "I pulled up to this apartment (or house) and these 4 or 5 guys jumped out and ran into that apartment and they're still there, I can see them partying."

Chuck: "How much did they take you for?"

Rookie: "$5.00" (that was a fairly significant fare in the late 60's

Chuck: Removes his coat and hat. "Stay here." he would instruct the rookie. Chuck would enter the house or apartment without knocking.

Rookie: He hears a woman scream. He hears glass breaking and the sounds of things smashing and breaking. A man in a horizontal position comes flying through a window and landed motionless in the snow. The sounds of mayhem continue and the sounds of fists hitting faces and other body parts continue. Eventually there is quietness from the residence. Chuck walks out disheveled, holding a fistful of bills. He walks to the car of the rookie and peels off a five dollar bill and tells the driver to leave, which he gladly does. Chuck pockets the rest of the bills in his pocket, eventually he leaves as well.

Chuck drove a two tone brown Eldorado. At night he would cruise around monitoring the drivers over his taxi radio. He was mostly on the lookout for drivers who were stealing fares. They did this by _not_ turning the meter on once they picked up a street fare who had flagged them down. So, how did Chuck spot these thieves stealing fares? How did he see inside a dark vehicle from a significant distance away, at night?! Well, on the roof of every cab is a plastic taxi sign, at the top of which, is a bright white light, which comes on when the meter is turned on. If there are people in the taxi, but no white light is on, that means the meter is off. Hence, the driver has not reported the fare to the dispatcher. Hence, the driver is keeping the money for himself. Hence, he is stealing the fare.

If Chuck happened to spot one of his cars with a passenger or two on board, but, with no bright white light on the plastic taxi sign, Chuck would cross the path of the cab, forcing it to screech to a stop. When Chuck reached the driver's door, if it wasn't winter, he would reached in through the open window and violently pull the driver out from behind the wheel and smash him on the hood of his car and beat him. Even if, or when, there was an old lady on board, his fist didn't slow down as he carried on the merciless beatings. Without missing a punch, Chuck continued as normal brandishing a forced smile on his face and through clenched teeth, would say to the customer in the back seat, "Don't worry ma'am there's another car on the way for ya!" The beaten driven would slide off the hood of the taxi at which point Chuck would collect every dime from the driver's pockets, including his wrist watch, rings, or anything else of value. Sometimes that included newer items of clothing such as jackets, shoes, or boots. Nobody screwed around with Chuck and I have to say I never saw him lose a fight.

I remember the time when I was being trained for the position of dispatcher by Chuck himself. Remember, Chuck was an intimidating character who was subject to bouts of rage when things became challenging. He wasn't known as a man of patience and I knew if I was slow to catch on I might get attacked and booted out of the building. Therefore, I was already nervous and tense before I even started the training session. As violent and loud as he could get, Chuck had a crackerjack sense of humor. Though he wasn't trying to be funny when we first sat down in the dispatch office, Chuck told me to be calm and that he was going to reveal to me the correct way to dispatch. With all do sincerity and in a solemn voice, as if he was going to reveal a divine truth to me, so profound, that, the entire scope and knowledge of dispatching would instantly fall upon me.

I took a deep breath, wiped my brow, sat up and listened as carefully as I possibly could and this is what Chuck delivered to me. "Remember Emile, the only thing you need to know about all those drivers out there is that they can't think." It was the most matter of fact declaration I had ever heard anyone speak. There was no slap on the back, gotcha, followed by loud laughter. It was an extremely low key delivery which made it even funnier. He really believed that what he was saying was fact. "*You* have to think for them!" He said with emphasis. "You are the pilot; they are simply mindless robots who were born without a brain. And so my training began. Now, I have to say, that eventually, I roared with laughter. Soon, Chuck joined in, breaking the tension that had existed before his lesson on driver mentality began. As I sat behind the microphone, I tried to keep up with all the drivers as they called in, whether it was to clear their fares, report their pickups, or ask for certain instructions. I was struggling to keep up, and, I must say, with not much success. Finally, seeing my difficulty, Chuck leaned over and placed his huge hand over the microphone and said, "Don't try to answer every one. Just answer one driver at a time. Don't worry about missing someone, because if you forget someone, they will call you again. Then you can catch them the second time they call in." That bit of information worked like magic and the rest of my shift unfolded perfectly, not only for that first shift but forever since that moment. With Chuck cracking me up, relieving any tension I had, plus, his constant puns and jokes relating to the cab industry, I enjoyed my shift immensely and I saw Chuck in a completely different light. He was a down to earth, likeable man, until you crossed him. He called a spade a spade. He was a man of integrity who thrived on honesty and fair play. But cross him, cheat him or cost him money and he retaliated and demanded restitution, first by asking, then by taking.

In spite of Chuck's fiery temper and violent tantrums, drivers still did things to antagonize him. In the early days Chuck kept a pop cooler in the office, not necessarily to provide a source for refreshment for the drivers and office staff, but mostly to make extra money. This was the type of cooler that held glass bottled drinks where the necks of the bottles protruded above steel rails. That meant that you had to deposit your money before the mechanism would open, releasing the trapped bottles. In no time, the drivers learned how to beat the machine. They simply used a bottle opener to remove the cap and then inserted straws to drain the bottles. The first morning Chuck discovered this infraction he wheeled the drink cooler out onto the parking lot where he used a sledge hammer to completely destroy it beyond recognition. Everyone who witnessed the scene laughed hysterically.

It was years, before Chuck installed any other type of beverage dispensing machine for the same reasons he did with the soft drink machine. Forgetting the fiasco with the pop cooler Chuck decided to install an automatic coin operated coffee dispenser for the office.

A week later the old boys in the office learned that by using a wooden ruler if you inserted it deep enough and at the right angle the cup would drop in its proper position and the coffee would instantly fill the cup. On Monday morning of a long week-end, Chuck came in and discovered all the empty coffee cups overflowed the garbage can as well as empty coffee bags, yet there was not a dime in the coin receptacle. Chuck roared out of the office with the entire coffee machine, smashing it to the earth with all his strength. He then jumped into his El Dorado and ran over the fragments, over and over, until there was no trace of a coffee cup anywhere in the lot. The dispatcher and a few drivers laughed themselves sick but managed to leave before Chuck returned.

The incident I found most hilarious was when some nervy driver used the phone in the office lobby to call his sweetheart in Green Bay, Wisconsin. The call lasted over 2 hours and when the bill came in the mail there was a three hundred dollar charge attached to it. That red phone had been a fixture in the office for fifteen years before I started driving for Red Patch. When Chuck cast his eyes across that phone bill he immediately let out a booming litany of colorful curse words and a slew of threats on whoever was responsible. He then sprang from behind his desk, stomped into the lobby and proceeded to rip the entire phone off the wall. In a sustained rage, Chuck smashed the item to the floor repeatedly until there wasn't a piece left that was big enough for him to

16

grab. He vowed that from that moment on, that there would never again be a phone in the lobby for the drivers to use, and from that point on, there never was.

For a long while, in the early morning hours, you could hear the roar of cab drivers at the Salisbury House as they recounted the scene of Chuck ripping the phone off the wall in the office, because of the outrageous phone bill some driver had the nerve to make. It took some time but the office manager took it upon himself to track down the driver who placed that call. When the manager informed Chuck who the culprit was, Chuck instructed him to say nothing about it. He instructed the manager to have the driver work as much overtime as possible and hold his pay for weeks, explaining that there was an office error and he would get his money next week, or the week after that. When the crook's pay reached the amount of the phone bill, Chuck told him to meet him in the garage to receive his pay. Chuck paid him alright with a grand slam beating attested by 4 broken ribs, two black eyes and a jaw broken in 3 places. And, oh ya, an empty wallet.

Only once did I see Chuck run from a fight so you can imagine the size of the guy. One afternoon a driver asked Chuck, who was assisting the dispatcher, if he could step out to use a wash room. Chuck did more than yell at him, he demeaned him speaking to him in a very patronizing manner. "Are you a little kid that you can't hold your pee? Wait until we're caught up before you go!" With that the driver grabbed his mike and roared his own response. "Chuck!" He said, "I'm coming to the office and when I get there I'm going to punch your lights out!" Immediately, Chuck rushed out of the office and peeled off the lot spewing rocks and gravel in his wake. A few minutes later this huge middle aged man walked in huffing and puffing. "Where the blankety blank is Chuck?" he bellowed. The dispatcher turned his head in the direction of this hulk of a man, who looked ready to kill someone. "He took off" Answered the dispatcher. This response didn't appease this fuming driver. He walked to the closed door of the woman's wash room and punched the door so hard that his arm crashed through the door until the hole reached his arm pit. Then he walked over to the men's wash room and did the same thing. He then turned to the dispatcher and said, "That was for Chuck. If he wants to talk to me about damages, tell him to call me and I will discuss a payment plan of my own which I know he can't afford!" And with that, he stomped out of the office and went back to work. Everyone was in awe. You did not see that scenario very often. There once was a driver who worked for us who was too tall for the R.C.M.P. When I entered the garage one morning Chuck was chasing him around with a ball peen hammer. I immediately spun on my heels and walked right back outside. I have no idea what happened and I didn't want to know. I only knew that I didn't want to be involved in a homicide investigation.

Another golden memory of mine happened when I was washing my car prior to starting my day. It was 4 a.m. and Chuck walked in. I was always nervous around Chuck because of his fiery unpredictable temper. I continued washing the vehicle avoiding eye contact as much as possible. On the wall behind the wash hose was an old sink which looked filthy at the moment because of the thick black grease and dirt stains that ran over it. Sure enough, Chuck walked up to me which I took as a cue to shut off washer so I could hear what he had to say. He started speaking to me in a whisper and calling me by name. "Emile." he said in a hushed tone. "You see that sink over there," indicating the filthy sink on the wall past me. I nervously answer, "Yesss." (I'm expecting something very unpleasant to happen). I think to myself? *What did I do?*" Again, in a hushed tone, he whispers some important taxi industry revelation that I am about to be privy to. "You can't see it," he says even more softly, but there is a bull's eye on that sink that only idiot drivers can see." I look dumfounded, totally missing the point he was trying to make. This time his booming voice returned, "Because the stupid idiot drivers knock it off the wall, every day of the week!!" As I held my breath he then walked past me and turned into the office…. Now I got it. Often I would come in to work and someone would be re-attaching the sink to the wall or adding something to try and protect it. I am so relieved that it was not something I did to set him off. I just quickly resumed washing my car.

The Dispatchers

*D*ispatchers dispatch. They are usually the ones who answer the phones when you call in to order a taxi. They are at your beck and call twenty four hours a day, seven days a week. Sometimes a lady answers the phone but this mostly happens during the day shift. Dispatchers are an integral key in the day to day operations of any taxi company. Cab drivers, from which all dispatchers evolve, carry a lot of responsibility and must handle stressful conflicts as they occur. A dispatcher often faces more than one dilemma in an eight hour shift, especially on Fridays or Saturdays, whether it be evening or midnight shifts, because that's when all the crazies come out.

When it comes to the most outstanding dispatcher of all time, the name Charlie Lucas comes to mind. To my mind Charlie was the longest serving and most adept dispatcher. He was there when I started in the sixties and he was there when I left in the eighties. He was the constant star. The unique thing about Charlie Lucas was that he was severely handicapped. He had muscular dystrophy. However he refused to allow it to keep him from full time work. He also never allowed it to dull his sense of humor or to lessen his cheery disposition. He was always upbeat. As a dispatcher you had two ways to communicate with the drivers; via a foot pedal, which sat on the floor underneath the counter, or by pressing a button which sat on the counter within reach of his fingers. Now, because of his muscular dystrophy, Charlie had to press a button on the counter in front of him whenever he needed to communicate with the drivers. To execute this task Charlie had to violently *throw* his upper body in order to reach the button allowing him to connect to the drivers in the cars. He also had to use the same motion to write the trip information of each driver on a slip of paper, and then toss it in the appropriate box with the driver's corresponding number. So the job that Charlie did was a challenge to say the least, but he never missed a beat.

Over the course of the years that Charlie worked for Red Patch Taxi, the place got robbed, twice! Both times Charlie was on duty. Because of the location of the office and lack of proper security, it was very vulnerable. Both times, the robbery took place on the Sunday night, in the wee small hours of the morning. In both cases a group of armed men quietly walked in to the Red Patch office. One of the thugs used a sledge hammer to smash down a wooden door with a pane of glass in it. Then they quickly cleaned out the drop box where all the drivers had deposited their daily bulging envelopes. Immediately following that they slowly escaped off the lot and disappeared east down Nairn Avenue. As for Charlie, the men gently placed him in one of the parked taxis in the cold dark garage. Because of his disability, Charlie was virtually helpless. To the best of my knowledge, those responsible were never brought to justice. Charlie was unfazed to the events and simply brushed it off as amateur crooks, who were probably ex Red Patch Taxi drivers. The tender way they handled Charlie showed they knew him and respected him enough so as not to cause him any physical harm.

I was often sent to pick up Charlie and bring him to work. When I got to the garage I would back in and once he turned himself so that he sat sideways in his seat, I would get him in a bear hug and lift him from the vehicle and place him on the office chair, then I would wheel him into the dispatch office. This is the way I always did it. Chuck was the only one who would simply place his huge hands under Charlie' arm pits and easily raised him up and squarely place him on the stool, without so much as a grunt. Chuck was a very powerful man. Now, there were times, when there wasn't a man around to load Charlie up from home and take him to work for the morning shift. Believe it or not his wife was very capable in accomplishing that task. She would pick him up and put him where he needed to be in order to be transported.

I learned through Charlie that muscular dystrophy rarely occurs in females, though they carry the gene responsible for the disease. However, they pass it on to male offspring. For that reason, many, that is those who know, choose not to have children or even get married. I remember that Charlie's sister died some years later when she was only middle aged. Charlie was married to a lovely good natured, no-nonsense woman named Linda who stayed and looked after Charlie like an angel of mercy, until he passed away in August of 2006. I wasn't living in Winnipeg when he passed so I was sorry that I didn't get to see him before that. She told me what her daily routine was like, living with someone who had muscular dystrophy. As soon as she woke up in the morning, she had to move Charlie into a sitting position and massage his joints and help him with his bathroom tasks and that was just the beginning. I figure she was an absolute angel to have sacrificed so much for her husband. I remember one morning in early July I was sent to pick up Charlie and bring him to work. I did a double take when I spotted their Christmas tree still standing in the corner of their living room, fully decorated. However there wasn't a single pine needle on any of the branches, that were no longer green, just a rusty maroon color. The dead needles were in layers on the floor at the base, of what once was a pine tree.

As I wheeled Charlie across the room I commented, "Is Santa Clause mad at you Charlie? I think he missed your chimney."

"I was going to take it down" he said, "but hey, Christmas is only five months away so why go through all that work?" He said that with a cheerful, devil may care attitude, which gave us both a good hardy laugh. I felt that in view of Charlie's predicament in life, whatever his home situation may be, I loved him. To even think anything negatively about Charlie ran against the memory of someone who, I knew, was a great man. He supported his family and held down a full time job under adverse conditions. God bless him I say! A good many able bodied men I have known, never stepped up to the plate as did this great man. I salute him!

There was another gifted dispatcher that I knew who later became manager of Red Patch Taxi. His name was John Edward Skrypnyk. Ed was great at dispatching and managing the place, but his greatest asset was his ability to step into a situation where heated words or pandemonium was happening. He would use his soft steady understanding voice, and in just a few short minutes the situation would be under control. With clear precise instructions Ed would have everything running smooth and calm again. He knew how to see the heart of the chaos and was able to dispatch effective solutions. He made it look effortless but it was highly effective. He worked almost every week-end. Unfortunately, he had a falling out with Chuck and that was the end of Ed but it was a good long run as far as it lasted. He was a man who was always cool, calm and collected. Ed passed away May of 2011 and I still admire his abilities and I was saddened by his demise. His wife backed him up whole heartedly when there was conflict between her husband and Chuck. She fought right alongside him. Dispatching can be a thankless effort but somehow the super humans needed to do the job always manage to show up and get the tasks done.

Another such super star was a man I only remember as Gordy. He dispatched and carried out his job with great energy and zeal. He was a true ambassador for the company and his greatest gift was his ability to handle and promote customer satisfaction.

Many times while I was transporting customers in my car, they would say, someone should tell him he's in the wrong line of work. "That guy should be a radio announcer!" I remember on so many occasions as I was driving some clients to their destinations, that they would express their fascination hearing Gordy speak over the air and commented that he must be exhausted once he gets home from work. While it's true that Gordy had the gift of gab. Even more gifted, was Gordy at handling customers. I remember customers who waited from half to a full hour for a cab to show up. They would be furious. Amazingly, they would wait, because once they got into the taxi, Gordy addressed them with admiration and gratitude and called them by their first names. Then he would sternly instruct the driver to "light Billy's cigar and give him a gentle ride home. Billy's been waiting a long time for Red Patch. Way to go Billy. You are the kind of customers we dream of having. Catch a good night's sleep Billy" Gordy made it personal and it worked. He kept the customers happy because he made them feel important, and so they remained loyal to us. He was dynamite. Unfortunately, at one point in time, Gordy approached Chuck and asked him if he would sponsor a baseball team he was coaching. Gordy mentioned to Chuck that each player would be wearing a jersey with the name "Red Patch Taxi" on their backs. He reasoned that since Red Patch Taxi conducted the majority of their business in the area, it would promote the business and heighten their profile in the area. Chuck agreed and Gordy went ahead and ordered the sweaters but at the last minute Chucked changed his mind and reneged on the agreement he had made with Gordy. This infuriated Gordy and he instantly resigned, but not before he wrote Chuck a long poignant resignation letter. Chuck never read it and Gordy walked away from Red Patch for good. I, for one, was sorry to see him go. It was a sad day for Red Patch Taxi but Chuck was the boss. It was a sad loss for the company.

Yes, dispatchers came and went at Red Patch. Some were golden, some were not, but all were unique. Some dispatchers fed certain drivers more than others which means they gave them the best trips. It wasn't necessarily because they liked one more than another, although certain female drivers seemed to attract more positive attention. In most cases the drivers who excelled in their ability in the discharge of their duties, make the job easier for the dispatchers. A driver who never got lost, arrived at the caller's home quickly, always caught the praise of the man behind the mike, more effectively than a driver who tried to butter up the dispatcher by showering him or her with coffee or donuts. Proficiency won every time, more than kissing up to the boss. Sometimes, drivers who felt that the dispatchers were blatantly showing favoritism they would storm into the office and confront him or her. Sometimes the exchange got very heated. I remember a dispatcher named Ricky who experienced such an episode, but, in this instance, Ricky was totally innocent. There were times when favoritism really happened, while at other times, it was imagined. One day this particular driver felt he was getting passed over, one too many times and eventually exploded. He stormed into the dispatch office and confronted the dispatcher. Ricky endured his outlandish accusations and taunts, for a while, then Ricky lost it too. Ricky was about thirty years old and in top physical condition. He looked like a linebacker who could have played for Notre Dame. In the heat of this confrontation Ricky grabbed the driver in question and literally threw him through the glass window that separated the dispatch office from the garage. It was a short debate. For the longest time thereafter, Ricky's typical reply to drivers who had something to complain about was a standard, "All complaints can be settled on the sixth floor after midnight!" (Red Patch Taxi was a single storey building). The message behind Ricky's instruction was clear, if you have something to say to me, we can settle it with our fists after hours. No one ever complained again after the window incident.

On another occasion with a different dispatcher, Gordy, sent a female driver, who was new on the job, to pick up one of our veteran drivers from the Crossroads Shopping Centre. He was joking but the new female driver didn't know that. In a stern voice he instructed her "Be careful," he said with all seriousness. "This guy's pretty shifty and he's mentally unstable! Don't turn your back on him, he's got deep psychological issues!" Apparently, the message really scared her, because when she picked him up, she refused to allow him to sit in the front seat. Halfway to the office she kicked him out of the car! It was hilarious; everyone thought so too, but not the new driver. Gordy was like that. He had a hilarious sense of humor.

Another time one of our drivers, who happened to be a middle aged Negro man, was sent to the old Safeway grocery store, now a bingo hall on McPhillips, to pick up a boisterous group of wound up women. Gordy, in his usual chatty bratty mood, asked the driver if there were any winners in the car that night. When the driver asked the women if any of them were winners, the women were so loud and excited that it was difficult to hear what they were saying over the air. I laughed when I heard the driver responded in strained uncomplimentary exasperation. THEY'RE ALL WINNERS!!

Car Versus Taxi

I smile to myself whenever I hear people exclaim how expensive taxis are. When I first started driving taxi in 1968, the meter started at fifty five cents and jumped a dime over every certain distance. Anything over two dollars was considered a good trip or fare. I was nervous at first, being new, in a city I had just landed in. I always wanted to take the shortest route with every one of my customers. But, because I was new, and nervous, there were times I turned down the wrong street or missed the turn altogether. You would have thought I poured acid under somebody's collar. They would yell, "Hey! Hey! Hey! Buddy! You trying to rip me off!?" People accused me of intentionally taking the long way around in order to keep the passenger in my car for as long as possible. That way the meter reading would be more when I got them to their destination. I have long learned that only a stupid, narrow minded, cabbie would think that way. The truth is, an intelligent taxi driver wants to get rid of his passenger as fast as possible because then he is open for another fare. The more fares, the more money he earns in a shift. The longer a passenger remains in your cab the more of a loss he or she is incurring. For that reason, most cab drivers refuse to be hired out by the hour or take trips going out of town because then you have to come back empty. For the time it takes to run those off, a driver could probably earn up to double the income in the same amount of time.

I remember this business man in Elmwood who took our taxi every day of the week and sometimes more than once a day, except most Sundays. This gentleman took our cab to work every morning, and after work we drove him home. Sometimes during the week, he would take a taxi to go out to a movie, hockey game, or other sporting or social events. During the summer, or any nice day, he went to his cottage out a little ways past Selkirk. So on Fridays, we picked him up around seven o'clock at night at his home where he would be waiting with a load of week-end stuff to coincide with cottage life. Things like groceries, barbecue supplies, and swim wear. Every Sunday afternoon we picked him up at his cottage and drove him back home. He spent what I thought was a lot of money on taxis. He was a golden client and we waited on him hand and foot, year after year. One day, out of curiosity, I asked, "Don't take this the wrong way, Jack, I, for one, appreciate your business but can I ask you a question?" He leaned back toward me indicating that he was interested in what I was about to ask him. In a cheerful bantering voice he said, "Go ahead Buckaroo, ask away."

"Well," I stammered, not wanting him to be offended. "You take a lot of taxis and like I said, I appreciate your business. My question is, why don't you just buy yourself a car? Wouldn't that be cheaper than taking taxis every day? He laughed out loud, as if I had made a most ridiculous statement. He slapped his knee and said, "Son, I worked that out a long time ago. Think about it. First of all consider the price of a brand new car. Add in the cost of insurance every year; even if you don't have an accident. If you do have an accident the price multiplies dramatically. Then there is gas, repairs, parking, when you can find a place to park. Then there are the cops to worry about, not to mention possible car accidents. People get traffic tickets all the time which increases their insurance or their drivers' license which goes up every year. When seasons change, your wallet takes a beating. You need to winterize your vehicle. That means new winter tires, plus who knows what else. Even with a new car my vehicle might not start on any given day, which you may not have noticed, but there are more than a few nippy days in Winnipeg during the long winter months. Now you may need a tow truck, but first you have to freeze your buns off waiting for one to show up. If the tow truck can't get you going, guess what? You still have to take a taxi! Finally, after finishing his rant, he leaned back in his seat, shook his head, and said. "No son, it's better my way. No matter what the weather is like, I get a new vehicle, and it's already nice and warm inside when I'm picked up, right at my front door. I can ease my mind by eliminating all those factors I've just mentioned."

"I guess I never thought about it that way." I said. As a last ditch effort to shake his theory, I asked. "What if you want to visit Vancouver or vacation in France?" I threw the question at him, thinking that I had found a chink in his armor. His immediate reply was, "I fly out there by Air Canada, then I take taxis wherever I go while I'm there." With that final comment coming as fast as it did, it terminated the topic of our conversation. But, I had to admit, it was a rational explanation.

Keystone Drunks

There was a bar on Main Street near Higgins Avenue where a lot of bizarre incidences took place. I had seen a lot of fist fights and stabbings take place and other spectacles that were extremely violent but every once in a while something would happen that elicited a few laughs. On this night I sat in my cab next to the curb waiting for a trip when suddenly the bar doors flew open and a man and woman came running out. He was chasing her but he was struggling to stay upright and keep up the speed. She didn't know where to run until she spied a phone booth which just so happened to be near the curb on the sidewalk next to my cab. She ran to the phone booth with the man in hot pursuit. She got there first then around and around the phone booth they went. No matter how hard he tried, he was too drunk to catch her. Once in a while he would stop to catch his breath. At this point she would point at him and laugh, slapping her knee. After a short rest, off they went again. This went on for about fifteen minutes. Finally, in frustration, the man stopped and gave a huge heave on the phone booth. It toppled over and collapsed, crashing loudly to the sidewalk, folding into itself. There they stood, frozen in time, facing each other; glaring at each other, panting over twelve inches of phone rubble. At this point I was sure he was going to attack her. Suddenly she burst out laughing again. This broke the tension between them and he joined her in the amusement of the situation. Suddenly they embraced, roaring with laughter and walked back into the bar, arm in arm. I was heartily enjoying the event and chuckling to myself when something bizarre happened that capped the comedy and put the cherry on top. Just as they disappeared inside the bar, the phone rang!

Creative Crooks

*W*hether you like it or not, being a cab driver means that you are going to be beaten out of a fare every once in a while. The greener you are, the more often that's going to happen. In my first year in the business it seemed that virtually everyone was trying to rip me off. It took me a few years to grow a thicker skin and lose my naivety and trusting good natured personality. Eventually I became more cautious and learned to safeguard myself against these thieves. It's not that I'm slow. It's that there are a lot of thieves out there and some of them are very creative. Plus, they have a greater arsenal of tricks up their sleeves than I ever thought possible. Even after years and years of driving a cab, I am still, occasionally, taken in. Like the time I dropped off this beautiful, professional looking, well dressed woman at an upscale apartment complex. I stupidly waited for this good looking lady with the black leather briefcase, for over half an hour before I admitted defeat and drove away. I learned very early on in my profession as a cab driver, that this is the absolute biggest lie people use, and is most used so that I don't even get mad at the perpetrators who try to use them. I get mad at myself because it's downright insulting. What usually happened was, when I arrived at their destination, they would say, "I 'm just going to run inside my home and get my money. Then I'll be right back to pay you." Some would add, I'll slip you a few extra bucks as a tip for being so nice to wait." What they were really saying was "Because you're such a nice stupid man, I'm going to pretend to reward you by appealing to your sense of gullibility and greed." I learned to politely reply by saying, "No problem, I'll come with you and save you a trip out." This worn out line was used almost daily by people from all walks of life, of all ages and genders. This line was never used from new immigrants or people from any other ethnic minorities because they knew that even a fool or simpleton wouldn't fall for a line like that. Yet people use that bullshit line on a daily, and sometimes, hourly basis. There is no such thing as an institution or educational academy known as *The Stupid Academy*. Wait! There is! It's taxi driving 101. It's on the job training. You start out green. You get beat many many times, leaving you feeling like an imbecile each and every time. Eventually, you develop a super thick skin and learn to minimize being a victim. Forget the cops, they're too busy to trifle with such pesky, annoying, naggy, time consuming complaints. This is a school of hard knocks that is ongoing. This is Taxi Academy 101 where there is no graduation day because you are too stupid to ever graduate. Heck you could go a year or more without incidence then one day a blind nun in a wheelchair gives you that line and you say,"

Smooth Operator!

*I*t only took a week before one of my fares calmly beat me out of my money and smoothly ripped me off. It was my initiation into the real world of taxi driving. I was extremely naive back then, being fresh out of high school, and I was as inexperienced as anyone in life could be. I called everyone Sir, or Miss, and when people said to me, "I just have to run inside the house or apartment to get my money to pay you, wait right here and I'll be right back." I would simply nod my head in amicable obedience and say, "Yes Sir." And that's about as dumb and naive as a taxi driver can get. This guy was smooth and calm as could be. He didn't say, I'll be right back with the money. Rather, once I drove him to his destination, he said in a quiet, calm, easy voice, "I already paid you." This was a first for me and I stupidly argued the point with him. After all, he did not pay me. That was obvious beyond debate. I missed the point. I shudder now at my gullibility at this entire scenario. I still feel like a fool as I rehearse this story after so many years. I got the call to pick up my fare on a cold sleet filled Wednesday afternoon at the McLaren Hotel. I politely greeted my droopy eyed drunk with a cheerful, "Hello Sir, did you call a taxi?" He smiled as I dutifully opened the front passenger door allowing him to stagger and weave himself past me and negotiate himself into the front seat. I'm sure he couldn't believe his luck at getting the greenest driver in the city at that time. Judging by the wide grin on his face he gloated, and, without a doubt, congratulated himself at the ease at which he would be able to accomplish his fraudulent task. The fare only ran three bucks and he surprised me when he slurred, "I already paid you."

"You did not!" I foolishly answered in what I thought was a stern voice, which caused the drunk to widen his smile. "Yes I did" he countered calmly settling deeper into his seat as he lit up a cigarette. I reported the event to my dispatcher, explaining what was going on. The dispatcher told me to sit still and he was going to send the cops to take care of our inebriated friend. "Pay up or go to jail," I said in an angry voice. I thought those words were going to strike fear and regret into this loser. The drunk simply yawned then took a drag or two from his cigarette. He soon nodded off to sleep.

I waited for what seemed like hours for the cops to show up. "Finally," I thought, "Vindication!" The cops had to wake this guy up. The fare repeated his original lie. "Your taxi driver said you didn't pay him, "said the cop. "I certainly did!" countered the drunk loudly as he reached back to extract his wallet out of his pocket. He aggressively opened his bulging wallet exposing a thick wad of five, ten, and 20 dollar bills. The cop then turned to me and said "It's your word against his. He said he paid you." The cop then kindly and gently helped the drunk out of my cab and allowed him to walk away with more than enough cash in his wallet to pay me. The cops got back in their patrol car and drove away. The total time they spent there was less than five minutes. At that moment I felt that I was the new Manitoba Moron of the Month. Someone should have given me a dunce cap to wear for the rest of my shift but the pointy peak probably wouldn't have fit in the car. If someone would have said to me at that time, you're a stupid idiot and a fool, I would have immediately replied in my most defeated voice, I knoooooooooooow!!! This was my fist experience at getting ripped off but it wasn't my last. I was officially initiated into the taxi business. Read on.

.08 Aftermath

Sometime in 1968 or thereabouts, the government of Canada, in an attempt to get drunk drivers off our roads, introduced a roadside breathalyzer alcohol testing device. It was used to measure a driver's sobriety level, and they came up with an acceptable measurable number. It was .08. For the longest time it was the talk of the town particularly around the Christmas season. Drivers were getting nailed left, right, and centre. For the most part, the public was happy about it. Many of us were surprised by how many of our friends and family members were getting nailed with it and nobody was sympathetic for them. I met a lot of people who were now taking a taxi to work because they were violators of this new .08 law. It was a great topic of interesting conversation and many such lively conversations I did engage in. I never had pity for anyone who got caught driving under the influence. If you're that stupid or callous not to thinks about other people's right for safety, then accept your lumps; you deserve them!

One day in May, about a year after the legislation was passed I met a gentleman who told me that he was glad for the new legislation even though he flagrantly abused this law on an ongoing basis. This young man of about thirty told me that he worked as a pilot in Gimly, Manitoba; [a northern Manitoba town which held a military air force base about 100 kilometers north of Winnipeg] from Monday to Friday. When he got off work on Friday, he would meet up regularly with his friends and party hearty well into the wee hours of the morning. He said that when the party was over his buddies, literally carried him to his car and sat him behind the wheel, and sent him on his way home. Though he was too drunk to walk, he drove himself home to Winnipeg, about an hour away. He said he did this for years! He said it was a miracle that he didn't kill himself or somebody else and was in awe that he didn't get stopped at these roadside breathalyzer checkpoints. He said that he agreed with and supported this new law and I would guess by his conversation with me, that he no longer practiced his dangerous habit. Whether he did or not, I had no way of telling, but I'd like to think so. He did strike me as a sincere individual who finally understood the severity of the alcohol driving issue. I know I could have been fooled, but if I had to bet on it, I think that he became more responsible than he had been for years. Who knows?

Cowboy Kojack

When I tell people that I drove a taxi in the city of Winnipeg for about twenty plus years, they usually say, "Boy, you must have seen a lot of whack jobs over the years! While it's true that I have run into some very strange and colorful characters from time to time, what people don't realize is that some of those *"wack jobs"* are the ones driving the cabs, not to mention the ones who run the companies. Although the term, *whack job* may be a little too harsh, perhaps it would be more appropriate to use the word charismatic to describe most of the characters I have met? I drove cab in the mid seventies when the series "Kojak" starring, Telly Savalas, was the number one cop show on television. Telly Savalas was bald, chunky, and always had a lollypop in his mouth. He was the first detective to use a magnetic, flashing police emergency light which he would stick to the roof of his car, while on route to his destination. When he would arrive at his destination, he would pull into the driveway or on the lawn at a 45 degree angle as if it was such a dire emergency that he didn't see the need to park properly.

One of our drivers who, was very much enthralled with the character of that show, carried out his driving duties with that same adventurous spirit of the show in mind. This driver wore tight leather gloves, the kind golfers wear, and a red silk bandana tied around his neck, kind of like the western cowboy heroes wore in the 1950s, like Roy Rogers who every kid in America idolized at that time.

Whenever the dispatcher sent him on a trip, it was like he was being sent on an emergency "Mission Impossible" type call. Immediately he underwent a complete personality shift and his demeanor would make a dramatic change. First, he would adjust his black cowboy hat, then he would place his hands perfectly at the ten and two position on the steering wheel, and off he would scoot. Unlike Kojak, this character was lean and long with a full head of hair. Like Kojak, he had one of those red, magnetic, flashing, emergency lights that he attached to the roof of his cab. Once he arrived at the customer's house he didn't just pull into the driveway like a normal cab driver would do. No, he had to pull in at an angle across the client's lawn announcing that the cavalry had arrived to rescue them and take them to their destination. The people naturally got startled and wound up phoning our office. They would scream at the dispatcher and ask him why he had sent the cops to their house when all they wanted was a taxi? "What are you going to send me next time I call a cab, the fire wagon or an ambulance? Get that idiot off my lawn! NOW!"

Yes, he was reamed out by the management for his antics and given a stiff warning, but to no avail. He was told to ditch the red police emergency light but he could keep the cowboy hat and gloves which worked well for a while. However, the following Friday, Cowboy Kojak repeated his antics thinking that by switching his red flashing light for an orange one, that it would be acceptable. This time management simply gave him the address of our competitors.

Ghoulish Discovery

There came a time when I was given the opportunity to buy my own cab with the company I had always driven for. I was very excited about that. With my being an owner it became my responsibility to hire my own drivers. I placed an ad in the paper and hired a young, clean cut twenty five year old man. He was a great driver who had no problem driving nights. He seemed somewhat nervous to me but I figured it was because he was just young and inexperienced, which turned out to be true. Everything moved along smoothly until one cold, stormy, late October Friday night. It was what I later labeled a Steven King night. The cold rain pounded the earth with a fury seldom seen. The wind joined in and blew mercilessly, adding to the mayhem. Because of the adverse weather conditions, the taxi business became extremely busy. Rain is always the taxi driver's best friend in terms of being lucrative. No one likes walking around in wet clothes especially with a strong wind on your back that will chill you to the bone.

It just so happened for this newbie that the storm persisted until the wee small hours of the morning. It wasn't until near the end of his shift that my driver had the opportunity to take a break. He swung past a Tim Horton's, picked up a large coffee, donut and a carrot muffin, Then he found a little nook on the side of a the Safeway parking lot at Kimberly and Henderson Highway and rested while he devoured his purchase. He sat in his idling car and did his best to relax. Behind that Safeway store, there was a paved lane that formed a T where a row of tall elm trees lined the property. He said that with the wind blowing the branches of the trees wildly about, he thought he could make out something in the trees but he wasn't sure what because the flailing of the branches made it hard to be sure. He said that for a long time, he tried to concentrate but all he got was a spine tingling sensation that added to his concern. He ran off a few more trips in the area but he couldn't get the eerie feeling out of his mind. An hour later found him back at the same place. He parked the car a short distance away from the T laneway staring intently into the flailing trees, concentrating, trying to focus his attention among the wet leaves, which still blew erratically, and staring at the oncoming rain. There was something there but he could not determine what it was from inside the car. Finally, after what seemed like a really long time, he decided to step out of the car and investigate the matter further. He wanted to know conclusively if there really was something up there or whether it was just his imagination. Mustering all the courage he could, he determinedly stepped out of his car. He walked bravely into the storm until he stood exactly underneath the trees where he thought he had seen something earlier. Once he got to the best position of advantage, he pulled out his flashlight and shone it up into the huge elm tree. The bright beam shone like a powerful spotlight on a middle aged man swinging at the end of a rope, among the branches. The macabre sight shocked my driver. He instantly dropped his flashlight and fell on his backside. It took him a few moments to recover but when he did, he scampered as quickly as he could to the car and reported to the dispatcher the dreadful scene he had discovered. Immediately, the dispatcher contacted the police. It was big news amongst the drivers for weeks. Needless to say everybody kept needling him about it, saying things like, "Are you still hanging around"? Or, "Don't hang around the office if you want to make money." After a while my driver couldn't take it anymore, and he quit. I tried to tell the other drivers to layoff him but who could blame them? It's not every day you can *hang around* the office and spin eerie taxi tales!

Way Off Base

*O*ne early spring morning before the playoffs started I dropped off a Winnipeg Jets player at the Winnipeg arena. After the player left my car and went into the arena, I decided to go inside and get myself a drink from one of the soft drink machines. There were about a dozen or more players and other personnel sipping coffee and chatting up a storm. Among them was a sports reporter whose name I don't remember, who seemed anxious to make a name for himself. I lingered near enough to take in the good natured jocularity. There was a lot of teasing and bantering going on and everyone seemed to be enjoying the social encounter. I enjoyed listening to the conversation for about twenty minutes, thankful no one asked me to leave because I was enthralled to be there eating up the interaction, of the jovial group.

Bobby Clark was one of the roughest, toughest players in the NHL; certainly the most punishing player on his Philadelphia Flyers hockey team. Suddenly, this sports reporter blatantly and loudly asked the group if it was true that Bobby Clark was gay. Of the dozen people seated around the table, five of them were in the process of taking a sip of their coffee. All five instantly spat out the coffee, spraying everyone around them. Many choked on their hot java. Some went into a coughing fit. Everyone at the table was roaring with laughter. All scoffed at the absurdity of the question not to mention at the nerve of that reporter for even speaking those words. Things remained unraveled for some time before a lull in the conversation brought calm to the table. For a reason I'll never understand, the reporter took advantage of this lull in the discussion to repeat the question to the group. The most vocal of the group whom I don't want to name other than to say had played with Bobby before he joined the NHL, looked at the sports reported in the eye and said, "I don't know for certain, but I want to be here when you ask him!" And with that the room exploded in laughter again and I decided it was a good time to get back to my taxi. I for one wouldn't want to be there to hear someone ask Bobby that question, being non violent and all.

Spiritual Child

One of the eye opening things that I learned from years of driving a taxi in Winnipeg was that I had a chance to meet many native people, with their uncanny connection to their family members, past and present. I remembered hearing the news on TV, radio, and newspaper, about an adult native man who was brutally murdered. I don't remember if it had to do with gangs or drugs but I recall the act itself was horrific and ghastly. It had a lot of people talking about it at the time.

Early one winter evening in February, I drove a young family somewhere in the north end, a short distance from Selkirk Avenue. I dropped mom, dad, uncle, and four year old child in front of an older single story nondescript home, where dirty ice and snow covered the front steps. The front door was frozen in place which caused the people to enter the premises around through the side door. They were in a happy mood when I dropped them off even though they told me that they were family with that young native man everyone was talking about, who had been murdered. It was a dreary cool winter evening and I expressed my sympathy to them, drove away and soon forgot about the whole thing. Three hours later I was sent to that same address to pick up that family and drive them back to their home on Keenleyside.

The uncle sat in the front seat while the rest sat in the back. In a calm clear voice the uncle told me the following incident that had taken place in that home that evening. They let the child play with some toys in the family play room while the adults gathered around the table to play a few games of Canasta. Later, the aunt made a few tasty treats that they enjoyed while socializing. After that, the adults retired to the living room. They put a small tub of warm water on the kitchen table, sat the toddler in it with a few toys and left the child contented with his bath. The uncle told me the child was in clear view from where they sat. They could hear the child verbalizing to himself quite a bit. They glanced at the child continuously, feeling comfortable enough to continue watching television and left him with his chattering. When it came time for the visitors to leave they were amazed at the story the toddler had to say. He excitedly told the adults that Uncle Richard, [the murder victim, brother of the child's mother], had visited him. Naturally they asked the child a ton of questions like, "What did he say? What did he want?" the young boy said, "Uncle Richard said to tell mommy and daddy that he was okay and now living in a happy place. He told his nephew that he loved him and to be a good boy for mom and dad. He told him to say his prayers every day. He told him to pass his love along to all the family members on his behalf. Then, he left.

I could feel by the uncle's sincerity that it was true and not something the toddler was making up. After all, little children are naturally closer to the veil than most adults and are often more spiritually in tune. That story left me in a spiritual lurch, but a nice one.

BEER ANYONE?

*I*t seems that everyone knows that if you want to purchase beer illegally, or at off hours, just get a hold of a taxi driver, and he or she will know where to go. People seem convinced that every cabbie knows where all the boot-legers operate, anywhere in the city. While that is mostly true with veteran drivers, most would never venture to enter that enterprise for fear of being arrested, prosecuted, and eventually fired, from their job. Once you have boot-legger, on your resume, kiss your job good-bye and, in all likely-hood, say good-bye to ever getting your license back. In other words, if you don't mind the public humiliation and loss of employment, you might think the added income is worth the risk. It's not! It doesn't take long for a cab driver to find out where these boot-leggers are, because, on any given night that you pick up a street fare, called in code, 10-8's, they will be able to lead you right to their doors. Soon it becomes a feeding frenzy among cabbies and it's not unusual to make a dozen runs to the same address in an evening.

In some instances, certain boot-leggers were as busy as a regular government run beer outlet. And they wonder why they get busted. I remember talking to a cab driver who got busted for selling boot legged beer and thus, lost his job and license. He told me how this senior fare with trembling hands, and slurred speech, begged him to get him some beer. "He was so unbalanced, he had great difficulty standing. He braced himself against a fence and he kept heaving as if he were throwing up. What a pathetic bum I thought. He totally disgusted me. I rushed to get him his booze so I could quickly get rid of him. Sure I'll score that for you, but it will cost you $40.00."' The undercover cop gratefully answered with a hearty "God bless you" and handed over the cash to the driver. When the driver returned and reached for the cash, the cop, in one quick, smooth move, slipped the cuffs on him. That was the end of his extra-curricular activities and the end to his taxi driving career.

I remember a certain boot-legger who thought he could beat the system but he soon had his wings clipped. This guy was located not too far from the Louis Bridge, a dead end street off Sutherland. This guy built a thick compact shed that was difficult to get to. You had to walk through someone's yard then along the side of a neighboring structure until you came to a thick heavy door made of 4x4'S. Instead of a window, which was located about five feet from the bottom of the door, there was a small square rectangular frame just large enough where a 12 or a 24 pack of beer would squeeze through on rollers. All one had to do was give a secret knock on this rectangular screen for a window to open. A second later a voice simply said, "12 or 24?" Immediately a slot slid open for you to drop your cash into. As quickly, the beer instantly rolled out, landing into the happy hands of the buyer. In short order, the whole town knew about this particular boot-legger. Soon it came to an abrupt end when the sturdy structure quickly got torn down. The cops didn't allow this booming enterprise to continue. They simply drove onto the property in broad daylight with a boom truck and, in a matter of minutes; the structure was razed to the ground. I never heard of anyone arrested there or what happened afterwards. I only know they never opened again and the whole thing went away. Al Capone was the most successful boot-leggers I ever heard of, and although he became super rich, he ended up dead and, as far as I know, no one succeeded him.

Red Patch Moving Company

I have always felt compassion for poor people. I can say that because I was raised poor, and poor people do things others consider, strange, odd, weird, and sometimes, outright laughable. One of those oddities is magnified when poor people move from one location to another via taxi. I have moved people with the trunk of the cab gaping open so wide that I couldn't shut it. There were way too many household items jammed inside. A couple of mattresses strapped down on the roof. Add to that, a hound dog heaped on its master's knees in the front seat plus a canary in its cage on the driver's lap. Add to *that*, the family's Siamese cat yowling in mom's arms.

Moving is a stressful event for anyone to have to endure, but when you get a scenario like the one painted above, you have to ask yourself, how could it get worse? How about forgetting the baby asleep in the basinet on the floor of the vacant master bedroom?

I remember such moves, vacating one slum landlord simply to take up residence in another slum landlord's house. In such an incidence I slipped some cash into the husband's hand and forgot about the fare altogether. It was something that didn't happen often. I simply couldn't ignore the opportunity to do a little good for another human being. After all, aren't we all brothers and sisters in the eyes of God? That's one thing about driving taxi, opportunities to do good happen once in a while, when they do, and you act upon them, the feeling inside is overwhelming.

Case in point. One evening shortly after I arrived in Winnipeg, I was riding the bus home to East Kildonan. I sat on the first side seat anxious to get home. A very inebriated disheveled man followed me onto the bus, past the drop box where he was supposed to drop his money or ticket. He made no such attempt. He simply staggered past me and plopped himself down hard on the first seat to his right. Of course the bus driver knew he hadn't paid so he sat a few minutes but didn't say anything. After what seemed like a long time the driver said, "I'm not moving until you pay your fare." Nobody moved, including the bus driver. After what seemed like forever, a passenger stormed up to the front and paid the fare. He then briskly turned and went back to his seat. It seemed the entire bus let out a sigh of relief. As we headed over the Disraeli Freeway I chastised myself for not being the one to have paid the fare. I was ashamed for failing to react.

Red Patch Mario

Most of the entire time I worked driving a cab in Winnipeg saw me favor the afternoon/midnight shift. I said before, I could work any hours I wanted. Usually, quitting time for the night shift occurred sometime around 4 am when some of the day shift drivers started. Usually, by that time, the night business had died down and all the night drivers were exhausted and ready to go home. It was customary at the time, that we would ask them for a ride home. We would then slip them a five dollar bill as a thank you tip. It was a great way to ensure a fast getaway from the office and get home to our own comfortable waiting beds, for some badly needed zzz's.

On this one particular early Saturday morning, around five thirty, I managed to snag the last night driver leaving the office, for a ride home. It just so happened that this particular driver was the reputed speedball of Red Patch Taxi, but I was too exhausted, and young to care. Fast cars didn't scare me, besides; I had a heavy foot myself. What's the worst that could happen I quipped? That's probably the same thought that many people had as they boarded the Titanic. I almost found out that morning what that worst thing was when I spotted his Mustang, Mach 3, personal vehicle. Without hesitation, I threw caution to the wind and hopped in. As soon as I shut my door the idiot slammed his foot down hard on the accelerator spewing rocks and gravel in its wake. I could hear the stones and gravel splattering against the office building. I acted as if this was normal and I said nothing, did nothing. Seatbelts weren't a concern back then and the laws regarding them were years away from being implemented. So I ignorantly remained settled in, feeling comfortably at ease, under a false sense of security. We stopped a short distance away at the first set of lights at Nairn Avenue. This only took a few seconds. Thank goodness there was almost no traffic on the road at that hour. As soon as the lights turned green, again, he stomped on the accelerator. We flew through the intersection and over the Nairn overpass until we reached Watt Street. From this point, Watt Street ran straight as an arrow until it passed Munroe, about a full mile and a half away. I quickly estimated that we were probably moving at a speed of a hundred miles an hour. I hid my concern and took comfort in the fact that there was a police station at the corner of Munroe and Watt, hoping against hope, that there would be a cop or two in their patrol cars leaving the station for the start of their shift. At the speed we were moving, I figured any cop would easily be able to spot us and would certainly stop us, immediately! It was nearly daylight as we zoomed toward Munroe. I was filled with dread when I realized that there were no signs of police anywhere near that intersection. I realized as we neared Munroe that the light was green but we were close to a hundred yards away. There was a car stopped in the intersection facing east waiting for a green light. I feared that he was soon to get a green light and we would get a red light before we reached Munroe. Again, the fool floored the gas pedal at the exact second the light turned red and the driver on the left in the intersection got his green. He then started to move through the intersection. It is only by the grace of God that the driver looked our way and saw us dangerously closing in on him. A serious and deadly collision was inevitable. The driver braked which allowed us to swerve around him. The speedometer read 116 miles an hour as we flashed through that intersection. Thirty seconds later, on Sidney, he dropped me off at my front door. It took the fool exactly one minute to drive me home whereas, it should have taken seven or eight minutes to do that, and even that, would have involved speeding. I got out of his Mustang on shaky legs, and not just from ending a sixteen hour shift. I said with sarcasm, "Thanks for the flight, Mario!" referring to the famous race car driver Mario Andretti. Over time this whack job outran the cops on more than four occasions that I know of. Each time he would outrun the cops then he would find the nearest available phone to call the police to report his car was stolen. He managed to get away with this a few times but he finally did get caught. He eventually lost his license and ended up in jail. On another occasion I overheard the office manager trying to pacify an irate senior citizen who said that she and her daughter were in the back seat of this idiot's cab sobbing and hugging each other in mortal fear for their lives. Mario was travelling eighty five miles an hour down Higgins. I laughed out loud at the absurdity of it when I heard the manager repeat this to Chuck, the owner. He roared at me, "THAT'S NOT FUNNY!" I had to admit it wasn't funny. I learned long ago that people like this mad driver occasionally end up killing others but often escape harm to themselves. Sadly though, even some of them end up in the morgue.

Midnight Laundry

I remember this one regular customer who worked as a night watchman for Manitoba Bridge and Engineering. They were located right underneath the Arlington Bridge at Logan. This was sometime after the place closed down. He was somewhere in his late fifties. He was neat in appearance but dressed in plain cotton work clothes. He wore thick glasses and was well mannered. This man was a real gentleman but weird in that he had a strange obsession that baffled all the drivers. He lived in Elmwood not far from Talbot Avenue. As far as I could tell he lived alone and had no family or pets. Every mid afternoon one of our taxis would pick him up in front of his house where he would be waiting with a massive amount of green garbage bags filled to capacity with something, we guessed to be, his clothes! Together we would fill the trunk to maximum capacity, so much so, that I had to push the trunk lid down using all my strength to shut it. Then I loaded the back seat from floor to ceiling with more bags until it was impossible to see out the back and side window. Then off we went to Manitoba Bridge and Engineering. When we got there I helped him unload all those bags inside the locked gate. The guy then went inside the compound, locked the gate, and disappeared inside the lonely yard. He was the only employee who worked there and I never knew what he did there. The next morning after his shift I picked him up again and drove him home loading and unloading those same green garbage bags. I never understood what he was doing there all by himself, all alone in this great big place doing whatever he did in total privacy. This ritual of his continued with no variation, for over a two years, until one day, poof, it ended!

My wife was the last driver to have him as a customer. As she pulled into his driveway she was stunned to see an impeccably dressed executive like character standing with a brand new medium sized suitcase. This scruffy looking night watchman was now attired in an expensive three piece suit, groomed to perfection. He wore an expensive watch to boot. My wife said she didn't recognize him at first. She couldn't believe it was the same man. No drab cotton work clothes, no massive amount of plastic garbage bags filled with clothes. On this day my wife drove him to the airport. Nobody knows where he flew off to but he was never to be seen again. For all those months of driving this weird character to and from Manitoba Bridge and Engineering. A night watchman with nothing to watch and no work to carry out. All those months of tirelessly loading and unloading all those bags stuffed with laundry. She said he didn't even leave her a penny tip. The whole thing is an enigma. What was with all the garbage bags of clothes: or were they clothes at all??? And if not clothes, then what, pray tell. Where he went and what he is doing now I can only imagine but I hope he succeeded, in whatever scheme he was involved in. I wish him the best and I am not interested in knowing where he escaped to or from.

Backseat Battles

*I*n my many years of driving cab in Winnipeg it seems that unfortunately, victims of abuse in our society show that the order of abuse goes from children, to women, and finally to the elderly which is a sad commentary on society. This is not the norm for Winnipeg but 1 believe that it is the norm for the world, sad as it is.

Sometimes, especially on week-ends, violent battles could and did break out in the back seat of my taxi. Back seats make poor battle fields, because of the restricted space which tends to amplify the violence, both verbally and physically. These internal wars tended to go on for the entire duration of the ride. 1 would shudder with high anxiety whenever it happened, and wouldn't you know it, the warring couple would just happen to live at the furthest distance away from where they got into the cab. It was bad enough that it took a long time to get the fighting duet home, but to add even more sizzle to the experience; the powers that be somehow orchestrated my trip so that I hit a red light at every intersection along the way! At every intersection, when my taxi came to a rest, it felt like the end of a round in a boxing or wrestling ring. Only, instead of resting a few moments, the combatants interpreted it as a signal to step it up for another round of violence. It was as if a muted bell went off to start the following round. The war started the second the couple stepped into the back seat of my cab and ended only when they arrived home. When the rumble got too violent, I would threaten to kick them out of the car, then, they would be forced to walk the rest of the way home. Often this would result in an easing up of the feud, but often only for a short period of time. It usually turned out to be an exercise in futility. There are times that battles erupt in the back seat and can become violent and that violence can take on absurd proportions when fueled with passengers who are under the influence of alcohol or mind altering drugs. Add to that the element of jealousy brought about by cheating spouses and the results can mean blood, and, or, insatiable rage. This happens more often than naught and it's the hapless driver who has to endure the seemingly endless journey as he delivers the dysfunctional couple home.

Over the years I've had to step in between fighting couples many times and most times it was the wife at the other end of the abuse. I would simply drive the wife away to safety where the chance to resolve the conflict would most likely be fair and amicable, or at least, not life-threatening. Sometimes though, it is the man that needs saving! I have two incidences I would like to share with you.

(1) On this particular Friday night my journey started at the Number 9 legion on Nairn Avenue at closing time. It was mid February and it was a beautiful night, weather wise, as it was relatively mild and calm, but that's the only thing that was calm when I arrived at the legion. By the time I got there it was close to 2 am and a young couple was standing in the lobby waiting for me. The second they got in I knew there was something brewing between them. Even though it was mid-winter, neither of them had a coat on nor did they seem to care about it. The guilt ridden man was pleading his case to his sweetheart though she was too incensed to hear him. As if on cue, large flakes of snow began descending softly and lazily to the earth making it look as if a giant snow globe had been turned upside down, a sharp contrast to the tempest raging inside the cab. I sighed with disappointment when they announced their destination being way down Pembina Highway, about a forty five minute drive. The battle began with a vicious slap to the boyfriend's face as her voice, filled with gross curse words amplified deafeningly in the car. That followed immediately by an attempt to land a punch or two. The boyfriend had managed to hold her wrists in order to keep from being slapped or punched. She fought like a

ferocious lion, her rage not relenting for a second. She screamed at him to let go of her wrists. He tried to reason with her. He answered as gently as he could, trying to pacify her and negotiate a deal with her. He solemnly promised to let go of her wrists if she promised to stop slapping or punching him. She would immediate agree to his proposal but as soon as he released her hands, she would immediate slap or punch him in the face. And I kept getting red lights. They looked like older university students, neat and comely in appearance, though their behavior was irrational and unseemly. Every once in a while I tried to rationalize with the two of them but neither paid attention to me. This stayed that way the entire 45 minute drive. She punched, kicked, slapped, head-bunted, screamed at her beau the entire way home. The only thing the guy could do to avoid a savage beating was to hold her wrists. When he did so, she became more agitated and violent. The violent wrestling going on in the backseat caused the cab to bounce and shimmy. We literally rocked and rolled home. The rumble in the rear seat was often accompanied with the sound of slaps and punches. She kept screaming to be let out of the vehicle but he refused to let go of her wrists because he knew what would follow if he did. She nailed her beau as hard as she could and as often as she could with every opportunity she got.

Finally, we got to within a few blocks from their home. I stopped at my final red light when she ejected herself from the cab and sprinted down the street like a gazelle pursued by a hungry lion. "Let her go!" I shouted in frustration mixed with relief. "I was hoping you were going to land an uppercut or at the very least, instruct me to pull over so she could escape!"

"I didn't want her to get injured or hurt herself. I wanted her to get home safe first," he explained. He paid me then got out of my cab. As I drove away I spotted her rushing into an apartment building a good distance from her date or whatever he was. It was only then that I breathed a happy sigh of relief as I drove away. It was finally over.

(2) Violence and abuse, no matter who the victim may be, is deplorable and never justified. The victim, in this story, was a frail, elderly, passive man in his early sixties, whose wife heaped all three, forms of abuse upon him mercilessly, and regularly.

I have to start this story of this abusive wife by giving you the most accurate description possible. I need to illustrate the mood, flavor, and tone of the miserable scene so I can paint you the most accurate description. So, I say, think of the Tasmanian Devil as colorfully illustrated in the Bugs Bunny cartoon show that used to play every Saturday morning. Trust me when I say, that she bore an uncanny resemblance to this Tasmanian

Devil cartoon character. It wouldn't surprise me to learn that she posed for the sketch artists at Disney Corporation when they drew her up in the studio.

The couple in question were of Scottish ancestry. I can still hear her shrill voice as she rolled out her *R's* whenever she railed on him, reaching the highest level of character assassination inhumanly possible. Every Friday throughout the summer at around 5:30 or 6, I was dispatched to the LaSalle Hotel. There I picked up this couple and the abuse began the instant she got into the car. It was obvious to me that he had had a few beers before his wife joined him at the bar and now they were going home. He always wore a grin of self satisfaction as he clutched his 12 pack of beer. This drove his wife bananas. She instantly roared in his face calling him a worthless, useless, failure, as a husband. A loser, a good for nothing provider, a failure as a worker who only cared about his beer! She called him a drunk and an alcoholic. She said he was a humiliation to every member of their family.

This was only phase one of the abuse. From here she turned up the heat by spitting in his face which brought on phase two which meant violent slaps and or punches to the face, all the while rolling her Scottish *R's*. It was like background music to an action scene in a horror movie. The poor old man didn't say a word the whole time. He just passively looked out the window clutching his case of beer and puffing on a cigarette.

I drove as fast as I could and prayed for green lights. I wanted to get them home and out of my cab as soon as possible. Throughout the trip I could hear the verbal abuse continuing and I could almost feel the slaps and punches she rained on him. Once in a while, when the beating got to be too much, he would take hold of her wrists to ease the pummeling she was dishing out. At this point she would overreact crying out in an octave or two higher. He, in a tender, reasoning, gentle, voice would plead, "I will be happy to let go of your wrist if you promise to stop hitting me. After a minute of this reasoning she would agree to stop hitting him if he freed her wrists. The spitting and litany of verbal and physical abuse were never part of this negotiation. He always agreed to let her go. The second he released her wrists she would instantly resume the punching, slapping, and spitting. The episode would repeat itself over and over until we finally made it to their house. What a relief that always was.

I remember this one Saturday when I was driving them home from the LaSalle Hotel, I always hoped and wished that one day, he would haul off and hit her back. Until now he never did, so you can imagine my joy when he finally slapped her back. You'd have sworn that she got stabbed and needed emergency medical attention. Immediately! He barely touched her but she squawked like a dying chicken protesting the injustice of it all. Boy, you should have heard her shocked voice! She was dumbfounded. Her reaction was comical and I savored every second of it. "Long overdue!" I thought. She repeatedly shrieked out, "Call the po-liss, Call the po-liss! Call the po-liss"! At first I couldn't understand what she was saying. When it finally sank in I happily informed her that *IF* I did call the police, they would probably end up arresting her because she was the attacker who instigated this entire assault. Now she had another title to add to her repertoire of slanderous words describing her husband. Wife beater! Woman beater! Sexist pig! Wife Abuser! Wife Batterer! It was absurd! Absolutely ridiculous!

When I finally got them home, she raced out of the car, running off like a scared Jack rabbit. Finally, after countless scenes of these two characters I said to him, "Why don't you divorce the witch. It could only bring joy to your life." His lame response underscored his timidity and passiveness when he said, "I haven't got the heart son." Thankfully, I didn't see that demented couple for a little over a year. I almost didn't recognize them when I finally did see them again. Previously, when we left the LaSalle Hotel, he would have a 12 pack under his arm, and her, flailing away unrestrictedly on her husband; NOW, a totally opposite scene unfolded. The extremely abusive Tasmanian devil was replaced by a kind, thoughtful, affectionate, and loving wife full of compliments and loving overtures. I thought I was listening to a radio comedy program when I heard her kind, soft, compassionate words say, "Don't forget, darling, make sure to pick up a case of beer to bring home. After all, sweetheart, you work very hard and you deserve a beer after all the hard work you do every day!" I couldn't believe my ears. She sang nothing but lavish praises on him all the way home. I was totally dumbfounded! I couldn't even imagine what could have happened to create the extreme change in this woman's character.

Part three to this story comes yet another year later. This time only the passive Scottish gentleman was there when I picked him up at his home. I said it was nice to see him again after such a long time. I asked him how his wife was. His voice became melancholy as he told me that she had passed away a few months before. "An angel sent from God" he said wistfully. I smiled when I thought to myself that that could be true, after all He allowed Satan loose for a spell. I hoped this gentleman would fare as well as Job; after all he suffered almost as much, only for a longer period of time.

Heartbreak Blonde

I know a lot of blond jokes but I refuse to print them here because I don't want to come across as being sexist or patronizing. Besides I'd have to allow the same space for dumb ass men jokes. This is but another story that has no connection to any particular sex as a point of interest.

One beautiful warm spring day on a Saturday afternoon I stopped at the 7/11 store on the corner of Watt Street and Talbot Avenue, to pick up a couple snacks and a soft drink. Like usual, it was very busy, so it took me a while to get out of there. When I got into my car, I saw two young men at the pumps sitting in their gleaming souped-up hot rod that sparkled like a diamond in the warm sun. It was obvious that a tremendous amount of work had gone into renovating this beautiful vintage car which had attracted the attention of many people. A crowd of people surrounded the vehicle and I could hear a lot of oohs and aahs mixed with lavish praises. You could tell by the look on the young men's faces that they were friends, who had both worked long and hard, on this project, and they were justifiably proud about it. They wore their colorful silk driving jackets to accentuate their inaugural drive on such a beautiful day. I stayed where I was, enjoying the sight myself, of this beautiful piece of work. The onlookers peppered the driver with a lot of questions like year, model, and many technical questions which I know nothing about. The beautiful sunny day accentuated the excitement of the moment of the appearance of this vehicle, which drew so much attention, including the attention of the clerks in the store, who kept looking out their window and pointing. This excitement went on for a good twenty minutes and those two young men had their chests heaved up past the steering wheel as they pulled away from the pumps. They spun off the lot through the green light like a peacock strutting out of its pen. Suddenly a young blonde woman sped through a red light at the intersection and t-boned the hot rod, sending it spinning into the middle of the intersection, causing a lot of damage. I groaned in heartfelt empathy for the two young men, aware of how much work and time the pair spent on their project and now a tremendous amount of work would be needed to repair this damage. The guys jumped out of their vehicle and exercised a tremendous amount of restraint not to get violent with this young woman, who looked like a young mother. I saw one of the men clench his fist but managed not to throw any punches her way; though, in this case, it was probably, justifiable. I have to say that these men were men of character because even though they saw their hard works come to ruin, neither men cursed or violently lashed out at her in retribution. I felt sorry for the men's loss and sorry for how this woman must have felt about it. Her silence proved it.

Queen of the Bouncers

A lot of times it's a hassle picking up a fare from a bar but sometimes, if you have an ally, it can make the job a lot easier, and faster. Of all the allies I had, as far as allies were concerned, Dorothy at the LaSalle Hotel was the absolute best. Located a stone's throw away from the Louise Bridge, the place was a bee hive of activity especially on week-ends. Whenever I was sent there to pick someone up, I had to wade through a herd of patrons indulged in partying and socializing. Often I had to return three or more times to let the fare know I was still waiting on them. I soon learned that all I had to do was tell Dorothy, the manager of the establishment. When I let her know who I was there for, she would make it a point to hustle the guy out the door in a jiffy. Its annoying going into the bar several times to collect somebody who really didn't want to leave. They are the ones who strike up a conversation with someone every step of the way out. Dorothy was a large lady that weighed around three hundred pounds yet carried herself with grace and aplomb. She had a loud, vile mouth who everyone feared and respected.

With Dorothy on the job, she would follow the guy as he moved past the desk. I remember a certain man whom I had beckoned four times already and he was still chatting along the way. When he stopped by the desk Dorothy tore his head off. Her tactics were much better than mine for getting the job done. I could never get away with her methodology. With this particular gent she bellowed so loud that the guy nearly jumped out of his skin, as if someone had dropped a firecracker at his heels. "Shut the blankety blank up and get out of here!" she'd bellow. Then she'd point at me and said, "Your driver hasn't got all night to babysit your dumb ass! Now shut up and go home! He's just trying to make a living. If you didn't want a cab you shouldn't have called one, then he could make a living driving normal people home who really wants a taxi! Take this cab while he's here otherwise when you want another cab I won't call one for you! Now get the blank out of here or walk home! I will not call you another taxi later!" with that final statement Dorothy would scoot off behind her perch behind the front desk as a conclusive statement. Everyone knew you didn't give her static.

Most nights I drove her home after work and on one occasion I asked her how she handled a rowdy group of loud mouth trouble makers, a task that even men find challenging. Her response was enlightening. "When a group of men get loud and loose with their language, I approach the table and address the guy with the loudest mouth. I get nose to nose with the fool and address him directly. I immediately lay it on the line. I tell them in no uncertain terms, "if you say one more word and don't calm down immediately, you're going to be in the parking lot waiting for a cab and I'll make sure you're never welcomed here again! Do you agree? Yes or no!? Then I shut up and glare at them, waiting for his response. That usually ends the conversation." I certainly wouldn't want to cross Dorothy at any time and from what I had seen, nobody else wanted to either.

Dorothy, a wonderful lady, a cabbies best friend.

Tow Truck Redemption

There was a time in the 1970's in Winnipeg where, for some reason, tow truck companies were caught up in an era of aggressive competition for business. As is always the case, one company, whose name I don't remember, was considered the scummy, slimy, dirty dogs of the industry. It wasn't safe to park your vehicle in any fast food restaurant lot to go in and eat, because once you ate and then returned to your vehicle, there was a good chance it would be gone. Yes, it was true, that people would park at Wendy's, Burger King, or McDonald's, yet would not patronize these fast food outlets. Rather they would park in their lots and then slip into a building nearby to conduct some personal business. They also never bothered to slip a dime into the meter on the street. I felt only contempt for those people who, when they returned from shopping, would argue with the business owners and claim that they were eating in their establishments having lunch. Thanks to hidden cameras it was easy to prove or disprove If their claim was legitimate then the restaurant owner would reimburse their customer's cost. However, it was proved that most often the case, the people's claim was illegitimate; then the bogus claimants were on their own. After a while when the competition became almost out of hand, publicity had the public up in arms. After a while, the complaints fell on deaf ears and the vehicle owners ended up paying hefty fines for the infraction, legitimate or not.

There was a public outcry from every media outlet about this unfair towing practice and kept the public riled up. It seemed everyone was talking. Some politicians voiced their support for those victims of those dirty tactics but the support was superficial, nothing changed until.......

One very cool Sunday afternoon in early November I dropped off a fair at the sports bar near the Blue Bomber stadium where a group of hefty looking men flagged me down. My first impression was that they were members of the Winnipeg Blue Bombers because of their muscular build and the fact that they were all black. They told me that they were at the football game and thought nothing of leaving their vehicle parked in the lot at the Polo Park mall. They assumed that the tickets they had purchased included parking facilities which they viewed as obvious since all five of them attended the game; and the fact that there were acres and acres of empty parking spaces at the mall because it was Sunday and the mall was closed, caused these men to be angry and cursed a lot about these unethical tow truck drivers. At that time, the head office of this tow truck company was located on Higgins squished right under the Salter Street Bridge, at Salter just a few blocks north west of Logan Avenue. It was Sunday afternoon on an icy cold day with a bitter North West wind, and because the Blue Bomber game was over hours ago, traffic was light, it didn't take long to drive to the headquarters of this towing company. The mood in my taxi was toxic. You could cut the tension with a knife. I spotted the steel shed-like building scrunched under the overpass from a distance where I stopped, just before the iron gate of the compound. When all five men got out of my cab one of the men leaned into my window and said in a menacing tone, "You might want to leave now." Then he paid me and I drove a short, safe distance away, making sure that I had a clear view of the steel shack, as I excitedly anticipated trouble which I believed these tow truck drivers deserved. Nothing happened for a while then suddenly, a tow truck driver flew out a window in a full horizontal position. He was wearing a Blue Bomber ball cap which fell off his head as he collapsed on the ground once he landed to the earth. A few seconds later another driver crashed out the door where one of the black men pummeled the tow truck driver with his fist so quick and so viciously, that unconsciousness was instant. He stopped only long enough to allow the guy time to fall. For the next five minutes I heard a lot of crashing and breaking sounds but nobody else flew out the window or crashed through the door, but I could tell that a lot of damage was taking place. The crashing sounds continued for some time and I decided at that point to get away while the getting was good. As I made my way down Higgins Avenue toward Main Street, I looked to my right, down King Street. I spotted a convoy of police cars barreling toward the compound with their lights flashing and their sirens blaring. I crossed Main Street and continued down Higgins without being spotted, satisfied that their dues were up for collection.

Self Delegated Summer Holiday

I came to understand that life in Manitoba; Winnipeg in particular, begins once the snow disappears. I remember one year after a particularly cold winter, we got an early spring, and the nice weather stayed for a good length of time. It promised to morph into an exceptional summer and that feeling seemed to have been absorbed into most of the population. As you know, summers in Winnipeg are magical. It seemed everyone had spring fever.

It was around the middle of May. I was driving around Transcona one beautiful evening with my window mostly down, breathing in the warm air and feeling the cool exhilarating breezes in my face. My dispatcher sent me to the heavy metal wheel shop of the CN Railway to take an injured employee to the hospital. Transcona is a heavy duty train town and the building where I was sent was exclusively dedicated to manufacturing wheels for locomotives and other rail associated cars.

I know serious accidents can occur at heavy duty iron working shops and I felt a sense of urgency when I got the call, so I braced myself for the worse as I drove there. Some people have their limbs violently torn off when working around heavy machinery, especially when there are fast moving parts adjoined to that machine. When people get their hands, arms, feet, or other body parts too close to moving machine parts, the results can be devastating. I have lost my lunch more than once, looking at someone's mangled hand or skull that lost the battle with a moving piece of equipment. It was shortly after first break when it was reported that a worker had injured his hand in some kind of machine.

The call came in around six thirty pm. I was apprehensive as to what I would find when I got there. I pulled up to the front gate where an employee was standing with someone who had been delegated to escort the injured man and see him safely into the taxi, and see that he got away okay. The escort opened the front passenger door and gently guided the injured man into the cab. His left hand was wrapped in a thick white rag. A sling hung around his neck and supported the injured hand. I couldn't see the actual hand but the guy seemed exuberant about it, not like a man writhing in pain, though, by all accounts, it was a ghastly injury; one that would keep the employee out of work for a few months.

The conversation that transpired on the way to the hospital was somewhat interesting.

As soon as I drove away he let out an exhilarating whoop. "My summer holidays start right now!" he said, "This very minute!" He went on to say that he wanted the summer off so he could enjoy the bikini clad girls who bloomed so thrillingly in summer. He wanted to enjoy the beer festivals, the beaches, the endless parties, and all the other splendid things about summer. This young man said he intentionally injured himself so he could enjoy the beautiful summer time. He told me that shortly before break he convinced his buddy to smash a heavy ball peen hammer on his hand on a thick wooden block, so as to muffle the noise and where no one could see them. He said it took all his effort to stifle a scream. Then, shortly after break, he pounded that same hammer on a steel metal table and let out a good loud scream and he hopped around in circles, like a man in excruciating pain. The foreman took control and administered basic first aid. He knew by looking at the injury that he needed to get this employee to the hospital. There was no question that this was a serious injury that needed hospital care. He told me that the company itself had some kind of employee compensation benefit plan on top of regular government benefit plan. He said he was probably going to be earning more money from the compensation plans than when he was working. This guy was enthused and thrilled about his summer plans that he had set in motion. He was like a kid who was out of school for the summer. He excitedly bragged about it all the way to the hospital. He was bubbling over with excitement.

"I wouldn't take a chance like that just to get the summer off", I told him. "What if the injury got infected or took a turn for the worse and you had to have your hand amputated. Or, what if, later on in life, arthritis kicks in and you end up suffering in excruciating pain for years?" I gave him all these hypothetical scenarios but to no avail. He dismissed them all in an offhanded way without hesitation. He was convinced that all would be well and he wouldn't allow these thoughts to impede his pleasure for a long beautiful hot exciting summer. Call me stupid, I thought to myself, but I'll stick to working honestly and injury free.

Trains

I've always loved trains. Even as a small child I remember watching the locomotives as they coughed out thick black plumes of smoke from its chimney as they left the rail yard. The scene always left me spellbound. For a kid living in a small gold mining town nestled deep in the woods of Northern Ontario, the sight was exhilarating. I still find the sight of a moving train majestic and thrilling. Of course Winnipeg is a train town where the sight of them is almost commonplace but one that still awakens the little boy in me. However, after living in Winnipeg for a few years and later, employed, as a cab driver, the luster kind of faded. I'm sure that waiting for a 250 car trains to clear a crossing for an inordinate period of time had a lot to do with it.

The Red River snakes its way throughout the city of Winnipeg. So do the rails of the Canadian National Railway and the Canadian Pacific Railway which explains why there are so many bridges. I lived in East Elmwood when I drove for Red Patch Taxi. I soon realized that train traffic at certain times could tie up the entire area in the East end of the city which caused me deep concern if I were in dire need to rush to a hospital. Remember, this was before the Concordia Hospital was constructed. There always was a higher than average concentration of rail activity throughout this area. There was a huge maintenance shop in Transcona. Heck. Transcona existed because of C.N. We were very close to Symington which was the main Diesel Shop. Many times I drove men and women to work at Symington and I was floored to see myself blocked from entering the compound because there was a train coming in or going out of the yard. I saw myself stopped at the main entrance for almost an hour at times. After waiting for this inordinate period of time and finally able to pass on the south side of the huge yard, you could see the massive, giant arch of the train as it was coming out of the diesel shop. On the south side on the right, you could spy the head engine and on your left, almost to the horizon, you could see the caboose. One huge, gigantic half circle of box cars. One time, the workman in my taxi saw that I was in awe of the sight and he quipped, "There are 250 cars on that train son. The distance from the caboose to the head engine measures a full mile". It was very impressive to see. While I appreciated the view, I didn't appreciate the hold up. For me, equally annoying was waiting for trains to clear certain intersections while transporting folks to and from the city. I remember sitting at the double train tracks at Talbot and Grey. I remember coming to a stop at the electronic flashing arms coming down and blocking my way. I remember looking way down the tracks at the in-coming diesel locomotive. When the train was outbound it picked up speed so that by the time the train was halfway through the intersection it reached full speed and soon it cleared the intersection. However, when the train was inbound the beginning was okay because when the train reached the intersection where I was sitting, it was moving at a pretty good clip. The more the incoming rain moved across the intersection, the slower it became, until it eventually came to a complete stop; and with 200 plus cars in tow, it took a long time. I'd then hear a clinking sound when the workers had to do some switching so they could move into whatever corral they were meant to enter. I remember when the caboose passed my intersection, being exasperated and thinking. FINALLY!! But No! Now another train was coming from the other direction with 200 plus cars attached to that one too. As I said before the only difference here was that the outgoing train accelerated as it moved out, so the intersection wasn't tied up for any significant amount of time.

One late afternoon I was driving a very pregnant woman to St. Boniface hospital I was stuck at the rail crossing at Talbot and Grey and of course it was an inbound train. The lady in the back asked me if l knew how much longer we would be, before the train would clear the crossing. l answered that l had no idea; but l was racking my brain, picturing streets l could take that didn't have the train cutting through, trying to come up with an alternate route. A few minutes went by in deep silence, then, the lady had a contraction! She loudly huffed and puffed which sent shivers down my spine. l decided right then and there to move. When the contraction passed l begged her, almost through tears, not to have her baby in my taxi because l wasn't a doctor and l wasn't intelligent enough to be one. l put the four way emergency flashers on and spun the car around and sped toward Gateway Road. "PLEASE don't have your baby in my car!" l repeated. She laughed at my reaction. She assured me that she wasn't going to deliver her baby in my car, which, for no good reason, brought me comfort, though l found myself hyperventilating and sweating profusely. l sped down to Munroe; cut through on Golspie to Watt Street. Then l flew down Watt St. to Provencher Avenue, then to the hospital in question. l didn't even care if the police stopped me for speeding, in fact they would have been greeted with thanks; but alas, none were to be seen. We made it to the hospital in record time and l thanked her for not having another contraction as l helped her out of the car and into a wheel chair. l ran into the emergency area and l was on my heels ready to sprint back to my taxi when she grabbed my arm and shoved a twenty dollar bill into my shaking hand. It's okay, it's okay, don't worry about it. She said "Thanks for getting me here safely." I spied some hospital personnel quickly wheeling her away. They were both laughing at me as they wheeled her in. I was not laughing. Suddenly, an overwhelming feeling of joy swept over me for the career choice I had made in my life.

Fares With Guns

*I*n my twenty plus years of driving taxi in the city of Winnipeg I never got robbed or threatened with a gun or a knife. I was a lot younger way back then and I was in top physical health with a wiry temperament to go with it. I didn't mind fighting when I had to, but, guns trump all other forms of aggression. Only twice in twenty years did I see a gun appear in my taxi from a fare. One was from a young woman and the other from a senior citizen who had recently been released from an American prison where he had spent 25 years for murder.

Here are a couple incidences that happened to me concerning guns:

Gun incident 1

One early July evening I picked up a dispatched fare from East Kildonan, who asked to be dropped off at a popular sports bar, way down Portage Avenue. She was an athletic looking gal about my wife's age. She was a

95

cute little thing, somewhat looking street wise, if you know what 1 mean. The conversation centered on the topic of the possible hazards of driving cab. At this point she proposed that we should stage a false robbery and split the take. 1 scoffed at the idea of a girl robbing a healthy, strong, "virile" young man like myself being robbed. (Yes 1 was a bit sexist at the time.) She argued her point and when 1 asked how 1 could convince any cops that 1 was robbed by a well dressed dainty looking girl. She immediately answered, "Like this!" and then she quickly pulled out a 38 caliber snub nose pistol from her purse. 1 tried to conceal the fact that the sight of the gun shook me up, and tried to appear indifferent and stay cool. 1 calmly answered that robbing me at this time would be a futile event since 1 had just started my shift a short time earlier, and in fact she was only my second fare of the evening. Therefore, it would not be worth the effort or hassle, since there would be little cash to divvy up. 1 was shook up but 1 managed to sound calm and 1 continued driving her to her destination but from that point on we changed topics. After dropping her off, 1 thought, no guy's going to take advantage of this chick. If any guy did, he would be in for a big surprise!

Gun incident 2

One lazy sunny afternoon in mid June, I was driving down Portage Avenue looking for flags (street fares). It was a nice enough day when an older man flagged me down at the bus depot, across from the Hudson Bay store. He wore an old, but clean, tan colored trench coat. He appeared neat and well groomed. He settled into the passenger seat and I asked him where he wanted to go. He simply said, "The Downs" in a raspy voice. I knew that he meant Assinaboia Downs race track. He reminded me of Jimmy Durante. I could tell by the weathered look on his face and his dark countenance that he'd been around the block a few times in his life. His somber mood caught my attention and I knew he wasn't a man to fool with. It was rare that I ever got a fare going to the race track in the middle of the afternoon. My curiosity was piqued. We started talking about his life and I asked him where he was from. It was an ice breaker, one I used daily in my cab. My guess would have been that he was a jockey; I was not prepared for his answer to say the least, when he told me that he had recently been released from some American prison near Detroit. His penetrating stare told me that now would be a real good time for me to stop talking. With a raised voice he said. "Look at me!" his hands gesturing over his entire body. "I'm a little guy! I don't bother anyone! Ever!" He paused for a few seconds to collect his thoughts. His voice took on a more sinister tone as he continued. Again, he reiterated what he had said earlier only now, his voice had an edge to it. His gestures became over-exaggerated and his voice louder. "Look at me! I'm small!" he repeated. Now he was yelling.

"I don't bother anybody, ever But, if you jam me up, I'll kill you!" His last words I took to interpret as a statement of fact. There was no doubt in my mind that he would in fact, kill anyone who would be stupid enough to cause him or anyone dear to him, grief. He was in fact, a small, wiry looking man and I doubted he would ever allow anyone to push him around and would not hesitate to overcompensate any opponent with deadly force. He continued with his story to explain what happened to him in Detroit, so many years ago. "A little over 25 years ago I was enjoying a few beers at a bar in Detroit. I was minding my own business when this great big Nigger (his words, not mine) picked a fight with me for no reason at all. He beat the tar out of me and left me crumbled up in a heap on the white tiled floor, like a used candy wrapper. "Look at me! I'm small!" he raved loudly again. Continuing on he said "So I waited for hours outside the bar in my car, alone, waiting for that man to show his face. And he did, once the bar closed. I watched him as he walked down the street along that brick wall. That's when I made my move. I stomped the gas pedal to the floor and drove my car right into him. His guts poured out on the sidewalk and he died instantly. There was no remorse in his voice, only vindication. Again, he repeated his threatening words saying, "Mess with me, and I will kill you! After his summation I nervously tried to change the subject. What could I say to that? I lamely said, "So, what takes you to the race track today? You enjoy playing the ponies?" it was the only thing I could think to say to get the conversation moving in a less threatening direction. "Yes, I do," he said glumly. "I was there yesterday and I hit a thousand dollar jackpot." Before I could congratulate him and take the opportunity to continue steering this conversation upward and onward, he continued. "I was on my way to cash in my ticket when somebody bopped me over the head and stole my ticket. Today, when he goes to cash in that ticket I'll know who that somebody is and I will empty my gun on him! I'll make sure he's dead before I walk away!"He then instantly pulled out what looked like a 38 caliber pistol. With as much consternation as I could muster, I said, "You mean to tell me that after spending 25 years in jail you're willing to spend another 25 years in prison over a pocket of cash." Without hesitation he answered in a raised voice, yelling his previous words. "Look at me! I'm small! I never bother anybody! But if you fool with me, I will, kill you!!" That was his final statement and I didn't want to continue this volatile topic. Once I got to the track, I felt a pang of sorrow for this man who had endured so much pain in his life yet never saw the error of his maligned personality. I quickly drove away.

Comedy Cab

*H*umor can be a great asset in releasing stress in any job and it's no different for cabbies. I always had a sense of humor but I didn't know how humorous I was until a short time after I started driving on a full time basis. Humor can manifest itself in many ways such as when faced with comic incidences, snide remarks, or sarcastic comments. They can, and often do, leave us in stitches. I was new on the job when I found myself driving one mid Monday morning. The dispatcher sent a new driver who was of Ukrainian extraction, to pick up a young adolescent Chinese girl. He was to take her to her family, somewhere in the north end, around Garden City. Our middle aged driver spoke with a thick accent. He was hard to understand because of his broken English! The office gave him the street to take the passenger to, but no exact house number. When he got to his destination he found he couldn't communicate with his young passenger as to find out where to drop her off. After many attempts to find out where she was suppose to go neither could understand the other and the driver panicked. As he tried to communicate with the dispatcher, his frustration level rose. So here he was, speaking in thick broken English, while the adolescent girl spoke no English at all! The verbal exchange with the office showed no promise of being resolved soon. The chatter on the radio was frustrating to even listen to. The young female passenger was crying in the back seat because she didn't know where she was, and the driver was freaking out because, though he knew where he was, there was no sign of the girl's family, and he didn't know what to do. No other drivers were able to clear their trips as the noise between the driver and the dispatcher rose to a fevered pitch. Finally, the office manager, with a stern controlled voice, took over. He came on the air and cleared his throat, speaking in a loud, and clear, voice commanded, "Relax!" but the driver went off on a tangent again. Again the manager tried to ease the frustration of the driver. Speaking in a strained, yet controlled voice, he asked, "What language is she speaking anyway?" "I no be understandink giurl! She be talkink Chinese, Japanese, Portuguese, or sumtink......" his voice rising steadily in anger with every word. It was then that I picked up the microphone in answer to the manager's question, as to what language the girl was speaking. Putting the microphone to my mouth I loudly volunteered, "Maybe it's English."

I never gave the matter another thought. The radio went quiet and as far as I was concerned, it was over and out of my mind. I went on doing what I was doing, which was probably reading my morning newspaper. Everything on the air was quiet for about nine or ten minutes. Finally the manager attempted to continue his deliberations with the driver but, as soon as he attempted to speak, I heard what sounded like a crowd of people in the background in the office roaring with laughter. This forced the manager to cease talking and the radio went silent again for another length of time. The second attempt had the same outcome. It took a few more attempts before the manager could take control of his voice and the uproar in the background had died down enough for him to speak and resolve the issue. The family had called the office with the correct address as to where to drop off the young Chinese girl. The help was gratefully relayed to the driver. Thankfully no one knew I was the smartass. I told my wife about it years later but all she said was, "I'm not surprised!

Paul Bunyan of Redpatch

We get a lot of people who come and drive taxi when there is a down time in their industry, like farmers for instance. I remember one winter this young man came to work for us, because it was winter, and he needed the money. He was about 25, very large and very polite and very powerful. It was always no sir, yes miss, please, and thank you, always spoken in a soft passive tone of voice, and always accompanied with gentle manners. This one cold Tuesday evening this driver had a fare to the north end in the dingier part of town and when he got there, the fare announced that he had no money to pay him. He calmly explained this to the dispatcher. The dispatcher told him to go back inside to search for a thing of value to cover the fare. So off he goes back inside the home to look for an item of value. He stopped to remove his size 14 steel toed boots and looked around. A short while later he came back out to his car and told the dispatcher that the fare had no item of value except for a brand new floor model color television set. The dispatcher flippantly told him to take it! Our young famer friend went back inside the house, removed his steel toed boots at the door, walked across the floor, and picked up the TV as if it were a toy. He proceeded to walk back to the door, setting the tv down and took the time to do up his laces. At this time the people were freaking out but they magically came up with the money to pay the fare. When the driver relayed the message back to the dispatcher he roared with laughter and said, "Good job Mr. Bunyan!" and tuned him off the radio.

Barter For Bucks

T he business of driving a cab is unlike any other business. You never know from one fare to the next if you're going to get paid or not. And if you do get paid, what form of exchange might that be. There is a healthy fish industry in Winnipeg and at certain times during the year I have been generously over paid with Whitefish or smoked Red Eye. The fare might only be three dollars but I would end up with twenty five dollars worth of fish. I remember people rummaging through the freezer of their fridge looking for something to cover their fare. Often, people would hand me a good sized roast beef or pork roast with a twelve or fifteen dollar price label still attached to it. Sometimes people paid me with beef steak or pork chops, a ham or simply with hamburger or frozen hamburger patties. No one ever offered me canned goods, but I wouldn't have accepted them if they had, because that would tell me that they were worse off than me.

At times people would roll off their watches and hand them to me to cover the meter. I would promise the guy or gal that when they had the cash all they needed to do was call the office and I would deliver their watch back to them. They had thirty days to do so, however, not once, did anyone ever call. I felt bad because I didn't need another watch so after a month or so I simply hocked them. Another time someone handed over a brand new snow shovel. Then someone put a relatively new hockey stick in my hand. The only thing people didn't offer to pay me with was beer. Of course that commodity was far too valuable for the customer to barter with.

Jungle Justice

It was about mid day on a quiet Saturday and I was parked across from a terrible hell hole of a bar that sat on the corner of Notre Dame and Princess just off Portage Avenue. I sat in my car reading a newspaper enjoying the lull of the day, when I spotted a wild looking white man walking north up the middle of the street, shouting incoherently at who knows what, haphazardly toting a double barrel shotgun. I was shocked but not in fear of him, after all, he was a good distance away and moving away from me. I wasn't afraid for my safety but for his. My first thought was that he had to be nuts to make a public spectacle of himself like that, especially in this, the most violent part of town. I thought this guy's going to get himself into serious trouble doing a stupid thing like that. He was walking away from me but he certainly had my attention. I decided that if he turned toward me I would turn and quickly drive away. I was still frozen to this scene taking everything in, when a cop car pulled up just ahead of me. He also stopped in the middle of the road. There was no squeal of tires or screeching of brakes. The cop, who looked like a veteran officer, because of his gray hair, got out of his car, froze by his door and watched this strange and potentially dangerous man, walking and rambling incoherently up the street. The cop took aim at the troubled man with the shotgun and in a very loud voice yelled "HEY!" The sound echoed off the buildings. The armed man spun around to face the sound. The officer instantly shot the man right between the eyes and he fell to the street. I was awed at the cop's accuracy but my thought was to get the hell out of there. I spun around just as another cop car drove up followed by another. I didn't want to hang around any longer, nor did I want to be subjected to any kind of questioning, so I took off hoping no one noticed the number on my car or the name of the company I was with. For the rest of the day I kept as far away as possible from the entire downtown area. I checked for any reports of what I had just witnessed. O my God! I thought. A man was shot down like a rabid dog, in broad daylight! I heard nothing on the radio, nothing in the newspaper, and nothing on television. Ever!

Puppy Meets Taxi

I have to admit that in my early years of driving a cab in Winnipeg, I had a lead foot. It took me many years to overcome that habit and change my mindset, to one of calm control. At the time I felt that if I wanted to earn a decent weekly pay, I could not afford to dawdle behind regular traffic when making my way to pick up a customer, or, to speed in order to get them to their destination. I wanted my taxi to be empty as soon as possible so I could be free to pick up my next fare. It took years, for me to learn that I needed the expert driving skills that most taxi drivers naturally morph into and do. Eventually, I did. At that time I did not think that my driving skills needed improving, but I had to ask myself, were they hazardous or dangerous enough that I could be led to hurt someone. Fortunately, I managed to avoid fatal collisions, but one day something happened that shook me up enough to convince me to take this matter seriously and to do something about it.

It was mid morning, sometime in early November, after I had dropped off a fare near Selkirk and Arlington. The dispatcher sent me to pick up a gentleman at the bus depot and take him back to Edison Avenue. Immediately, my brain planned out my route. I drove, (sped) down Dufferin Avenue with the intention that once I reached the Salter Street Bridge, I would turn right and drive past Ellice Avenue where Salter becomes Balmoral Avenue and continue until I reached Portage Avenue. All I had to do then was turn right, where I would find myself right at the front doors of the bus depot. Normally the dispatcher would never have sent me that far for a trip but he was critically short on cars at the moment. He knew that I was fast, so he sent me. It was a decent sized monetary trip so I cruised merrily along down Dufferin, feeling comfortable behind the wheel. There wasn't much traffic because it was a cold morning and it was sometime before noon. Back in those days it was common for dogs to run loose all over the neighborhood. Suddenly a medium sized, short haired, gray dog emerged quickly from my left and crossed directly in front of my car in its attempt to reach the other side of the street. I immediately slammed on my brakes and barely missed running over the dog. Being a dog lover I was relieved that I had avoided running over this gray dog. I had just let out a huge sigh of relief, proud of my driving skills because I had managed to avoid hurting the animal. That was a short lived victory! Immediately behind that gray dog, a dog half the size of the gray dog followed behind in a perfectly straight line. Him I didn't miss. I, again, slammed on my brakes. Then I felt a bump when I drove over him, causing him to let out a pitiful yelp. I quickly pulled over to the right side of the dirt road and hopped out of my cab. My heart broke when I spied that tiny puppy lying on its side. I could see the indentation of the tire tracks on the dog's body where my front tires had run over him. To accentuate my remorse and feelings of guilt, a young boy appeared at the dog's side sobbing, uncontrollably, saying accusingly, "You killed my dog!" By this time I was kneeling over the dog looking for any sign of life. A few minutes later I notice the pup attempted to get up. The kid exclaimed, "He's alive, he's alive!" I brushed dirt and gravel off the little dog and helped stabilize him as the kid gently picked him up. "Your puppy might look okay but I think you should take him home for your parents to tend to him and see that he rest up for a couple days. Keep him close to you when you go somewhere together. Keep him on a leash." In spite of my advice, I knew it was my fault and I ruminated on this incident which played a part of me to slow down. The thought came to me; this could have been a kid I ran over! This time I got off easy. I never wanted to ever experience this feeling again knowing that running over a human being would be much more traumatic and scary. I never wanted to hurt any living thing, man or animal. I never did.

Gone With The Wind

O ne morning in mid December I was dispatched to pick up certain legal documents from a lawyer's home on Gateway Road. He worked on the tenth floor of the Richardson Building and I was to bring them from his home to his office as quickly as possible. The Richardson Building was a somewhat newly constructed building at the time, which was the talk of the town. It just so happened that, that day was a miserable cold freezing day with powerful strong winds to make it unbearable. Sleet and snow pelted the windows causing the wipers to become covered with thick ice which made a racket as they scrapped over the windshield. There was an air of urgency in the dispatcher's voice that caused me a deep sense of anxiety to deliver those documents as soon as possible. I knew the time when I was supposed to deliver the items this early in the morning was going to be very challenging. It was bad enough that traffic would be at its worst, but finding a parking spot would be next to impossible. It was definitely going to be insane! I expected the worst and I got the worst!

It was about ten thirty in the morning when I pulled into the only parking spot that was available at the back of the Richardson Building. The place that I parked in said "Reserved" which gave me greater anxiety. The place was a zoo. People were moving about everywhere. I strained my eyes hoping for a long time to spot someone vacating their spot, but there was nowhere else to park. The wind made the taxi shimmy as if it was about to flip over onto its roof. I kept looking around for another place to park, but eventuality I gave up on the idea, knowing it was futile. I did what any desperate man would do under the circumstances. I lied to myself, convincing myself that if I moved quickly enough, I could deliver those documents and be back in my cab in enough time to avoid meeting up with a commissionaire (meter man). Like a fool convinced, I made my move. When I opened my door, the wind nearly tore it out of my hands. I had to use both hands to shut my door and all my hair instantly stood on end making me look like a scared porcupine. With my head down and my shoulders hunched like the hunchback of Notre Dame, I struggled with all my might through this wind tunnel. The wind blew the door out of my grip and slammed it shut so hard that I thought the metal parts had welded it closed. I ran to the door, ducked into the lobby, and ran to the elevators. After what seemed like a long time, I joined the mob into the elevator and rode it up to the tenth floor. I got out of the elevator and found the office I needed to find. I went in and delivered the parcel. The gentleman paid me and I promptly left, anxious to get back to my waiting taxi, terrified as to what I would find when I got there. The possibility of getting a parking ticket weighed heavily on my mind because I knew if I got a parking ticket my whole day's earnings would be for nothing. It means I would be in the hole, financially speaking. I waited a lot longer for the elevator to return to the tenth floor. I don't know why it is, when people wait on some electrical mechanism, like an elevator or cross walk, that we press the button over and over again like as if it would make it come faster. It just doesn't make a bit of difference. When I exited the back of the Richardson Building the wind had gained in intensity, ripping the door out of my hands again, smashing into a poor unsuspecting pedestrian, knocking him to the ground. It seemed to me that it had actually gotten a few degrees colder in the short time that I was gone. The man struggled to get back on his feet but the strong arctic winds forced his white trench coat to open, pinning him to the ground. As he sat up a bit the wind blew his fedora off his head and sent it spinning away in a matter of seconds. When it hit another tall building, it sent the hat straight up a great height and blew it over to the right where it disappeared in seconds. Good bye fedora I thought to myself, you'll never see that thing ever again. I felt the icy cold air biting my face, so I quickly grabbed my door and attempted to open it. At that exact same second I noticed a dreaded commissionaire writing me a parking ticket. It instantly raised my ire. I ignored the man completely and quickly hopped in behind the wheel. I slammed the door shut, keeping the cold and wind out. I quickly started the car and in a few seconds the heat started to fill the vehicle. I adamantly ignored the commissionaire who was frantically writing away on his metal clipboard. I put the car in gear, intending to drive away but he shouted for me to stay put, which I did. I was fuming as he wrote out the ticket all the while suffering through the onslaught of the icy cold wind and the freezing temperatures.

When he finally finished writing the ticket he knocked on my window and handed it to me. By this time I was in a rage. I snapped the ticket from his hand and shut the door of my cab as hard as possible. I immediately proceeded to rip up the ticket into so many pieces, that eventually I couldn't rip it up into any more pieces. Then I rolled down my window, stuck out my clenched hand, and then opened it, releasing all the colored pieces into the whirlwind. The freezing wind immediately blew it out of my hand and sent it flying upward into colorful confetti helix. All before the commissionaire's eyes, but I was too angry to care. It was then at that exact moment that I noticed a well dressed businessman walking by, laughing heartily at the spectacle. The gentleman tried to stifle the laugh but he couldn't because he was enjoying it too much. He just kept his head down and smiled broadly as he walked past. My parking ticket was gone with the wind but, unfortunately not gone forever. The thought still felt like victory and I savored it as one. I'll moan about it later when I get the notice in the mail not until then, halleluiah!

Yes, eventually I had to pay the ticket but for the moment it was the only sweet revenge I could exact and it felt good. Yes, it was worth it! My anger and frustrations like the confetti was gone with the wind!

Main Street Mayhem

*L*ike I said earlier, I was born and raised in the little hockey town in northern Ontario called, Kirkland Lake. Although I had many native friends whom I interacted with, long before I attended high school, I was quite naïve when it came to really being objective when it came to the issue of natives, or as most called, Indians. Which goes to show what happens when we let foreigners navigate the world? (Just joking) That changed once I moved to Winnipeg. In my childhood years my best friend was a kid named Birdie White Duck and we got along famously. I didn't see him as native or non native. He was just a kid like me; my friend. We made sling shots together, smashed a few street lights together, swam in isolated country ponds prior to the official start of summer, and scavenged through the dump looking for discarded treasures. It was better than, and long before, we ever heard the term, "garage sale." Once I hit high school, I made friends with aboriginal kids who were from the reserve. I joined the wrestling team and I met an aboriginal student whose name was Andrew Wesley. He was the all Ontario inter collegiate wrestling champ in his weight class for three years in a row. He was a great athlete and, a very skilled wrestler. We had great laughs together. He had a great sense of humor and so did 1 which cemented our friendship. 1 affectionately called him Kemo-Sabi and he called me Tonto.

And so it was that when 1 first arrived in Winnipeg and saw how aboriginals interacted with, and were interacted upon, at every level of society, 1 found it to be sad, and disturbing. It took me years to more fully understand their plight in society. 1 saw how violently the cops and other members of society, especially those in positions of authority and power, spoke to them, their voices filled with derision and scorn. It seems that natives were too often dehumanized and therefore thought themselves deserving of the onslaught of their indignant abusers. 1 met many police officers who walked a beat on Main Street. 1 always found it uncanny how those who interacted with the natives on an ongoing basis developed an inherent ability to parrot their accent and tone with perfect aboriginal diction. Cops were one of those who developed this skill. Others included cab drivers. Unfortunately many used that talent to mock, not to simply jest in good natured interaction. The idea was to not use that ability to mock or berate. 1 remember hearing people labeling or berating them by giving them names like Lysol Larry, or, "Slow Running

Water." Too often it was an exercise in scorn, laughter, and humiliation. I remember overhearing a conversation, while eating a meal at a Salisbury House restaurant. A gentleman in a brown corduroy jacket was reacting to a patron who expressed disgust over the natives show of public drunkenness, violence, and overall anti social behavior. In a booming voice he said, "How can you expect any human being who had been sentenced to live on a reserve in the Northern wilderness of Manitoba, totally isolated from civilization, and once they come into contact with civilianization, expect them to behave as if they just came from prep school. Of course they're going to behave in a manner that you perceive as uncivilized. Of course if you feel like peeing you will simply pull it out and pee, no matter who is watching. Same goes for sex against a brick wall, plate glass window, or under an awning. Same goes for violent acts of aggression. Why are you surprised when they react to the rules of the jungle! We put them there in the first place! We give them cash and stick them far away in the wilderness, out of sight from us, the so called, superior white man. How would any human being react any differently!? Why do you even question it when you see bloody fights, brawls, stabbings, murders and everything else that goes on"? The gentleman was on a roll and so he continued. "Don't you remember reading in our history books where it was quoted by one of our wonderful founding fathers that the only good Indian is a dead Indian? If you ever

119

took the time to study the exploitation and abuse of the true citizens of this country, by us, it would pale in comparison to Adolf Hitler!" He then quieted down but soon got up to pay his bill, then left the quiet restaurant. Profound speech I thought to myself and I never forgot it.

It's not just the justice system, or the government at all levels that add to the mistreatment of our native brothers and sisters. It's also the overall mindset of the average citizen regarding native Canadians which manifest itself through the actions of some people in our society. Let me illustrate my point. My old boss whom I worked with at Ray-o-Vac, out in St. James, (I will call him George) solemnly told me, that on a Friday or Saturday evening, he took his family and parked along Main Street near the chaotic bars, much as the average father would take his family to a drive in theatre. It was for purely entertainment purposes. They would then observe the natives all evening long. They enjoyed the hours during, and, especially, after, the bars closed. This was when the natives spilled out into the street when pandemonium took place. They reveled in the native's drunken behavior, and were very enthused, observing it. Where else could you see crowds of people fighting, brawling, vomiting, having sex, and who knows what else, up close and in living color? For George and his family, it was better than going to a drive in movie! Heck, they actually brought refreshments with them like pop corn, pop, hot dogs, and sweets. The scene, unfortunately, gave the observers a twisted interpretation on the reality of what they were seeing. First of all, not all indigenous people behave like this, and second, the real explanation of the scene can be best explained as a result of centuries long of a history of systemic abuse. It's not a coincidence that the vast majority of people incarcerated in our penal institutions are natives. Yes, they may be guilty of their crimes but we, (society) are, for the most part, responsible. Much more work is needed to rectify this problem but I do see hope. Nowadays, many aboriginals are fighting back by taking a position of strength, armed with an education, and therefore are more capable in articulating and negotiating needed changes. Suffice it to say, let this be the end to this topic. I still have good native friends today.

Shovelling Out Abuse

*A*bout a month after I first started driving taxi, I decided to work my first day shift which so happened to be a Saturday. My first fare was a lady from an address on Martin Avenue and she instructed me to take her to an address somewhere north on 59 highway and east of Bird's Hill, out in the country. I had never been there before but she said that she would be happy to direct me. She was dressed in a full length, clean, plain light cotton house dress. She wore her hair combed to the side with a decorative plastic comb stuck in it, above her left ear, which held back a thick wave of dark hair. I guessed her age at about 40 and she wore a modest application of makeup which made her look attractive. In our conversation to her country home, she told me that she and her husband had been drinking the night before at the bar and somehow, they got separated, and she hadn't come home from the party until now. She figured her husband was probably going to be angry. Right away my guard went up and I prepared for an aggressive confrontation. We turned East off Highway 59, then, continued east for another 10 miles on a dirt road with many twists and turns. At last I rounded a hill and passed the final twist at the bottom. It was there that I pulled into a driveway and drove up to a small one story board and baton house.

It was a beautiful bright sunny morning. A veranda stretched along the entire front of the house with the main door stuck right in the middle. Chopped wood was neatly piled on either side of the screen door. The husband, a lean and lanky fellow, sat facing the driveway nursing a beer. He sat leisurely on a lawn chair with a ball cap perched neatly on his head. The second I came to a full stop at the front of the house, his smile disappeared from his face and I knew things were going to get heated up. He laid down his beer on the ground at the foot of his chair then bounded to the passenger door of my car. In a flash, even before I could open my door and step out, he violently grabbed his wife and pulled her out of her seat so aggressively that it was almost comical, though tragic. It looked like her seat had ejected her from the car. With a wild backhander to her face he sent her reeling to the ground, sending her sprawling in a most undignified manner. She landed a short distance away in the dirt sending her dress billowing over her head, revealing blue panties. He was about to go at her again but I raised my voice at him and said, "Whoa, whoa, whoa. Stop that right now! I know this is none of my business; I'm just a cab driver trying to make a living. I just want my money so I can get the hell out of here!" At this point he raised his voice and asked, "How much is the fare?"

"Nineteen dollars and fifty cents," I replied. In shock he roared, "What!" Then he spun around and violently grabbed her, pulled her up from the dirt and gave her another backhander, sending her sprawling again with the same results. This time I stepped in. I grabbed him by the scruff of the neck and roared back at him. "Look, I don't want to fight with you but if you try that crap again you'll be fighting with me and not a woman and I promise you, you will have a more difficult time with me than with your wife. I just want my money. Pay me and let me off this Merry Go Round." He calmed down somewhat, and, with difficulty, managed to pull out his wallet, and handed me a $50 bill. At this point we were crouched down on the ground, facing each other. I was about to protest his offer because I had no change for such a large bill this early in the morning when out of nowhere I felt a gust of wind whoosh pass my ear. Something solid had zoomed past my head. I felt my hair parting at the top of my head from the gust of wind this item created. In the same instance I heard the unmistakable sound of a metal object connecting with someone's head. I could almost see the word BOING, like you see in cartoons, the word hanging in the air, as her dear old hubby fell and lay crumpled in the dirt on the driveway, totally unconscious still holding the $50 bill.

Because her husband and I got caught up in arguing, we had lost sight of his wife. It was then that I saw his wife toss down a long handled shovel and snap the fifty dollar bill from her husband's fist and gave it to me with the words, "Keep the change!" Mickey Mantle couldn't have swung his bat more effectively than this lady had swung the long handled shovel. I'm sure the shovel hummed like a tuning fork for several minutes. I looked at the poor guy keeled over in the driveway with my jaw hanging open. "What if he's dead?" I lamely protested.

"I'm not that lucky son." She quipped. "Now get out of here!" With relief I peeled out of their driveway leaving rocks and gravel peppered over the body on the road and headed back to highway 59. For the next week or so I feared that the cops were going to come banging on my door with a subpoena to appear in court as a material witness in a murder investigation. Luckily I never heard anything on the news. In my mind no news is good news.

Reverse Con

*W*ith every fare you get, there is always a possibility that he or she will rob you of your money, and I found out long ago, that they can be very creative when doing so. I have come to accept the conclusion, a long time ago, that it doesn't matter how many years of driving taxi experience you may have, how cautious or intelligent you might be, the chance is always there that you will get beaten out of your fare. All you can do is try your best not to put yourself in any vulnerable positions that put you at risk. When someone says to you, I just have to run into the house to get my money, you go with them into their house and say that you will save them a trip back. This is your best approach. You can do this 10,000 times and one day you get a passenger who seems professional, intelligent, and charismatic, so you say sure and wait like a dummy in the car and when they don't come back, you hate yourself but you don't blame anyone but yourself. I look at it as the cost of doing business. I imagine having this conversation with a cop (whom I would never call in the first place) that could go like this:

Cabbie: But officer the nice man with the Sear Sucker Suit said he had to go inside his house to get the money to pay me. He said he would be right back.

Cop: "Ha ha ha ha ha ha h ha ha hohohohohohohohohoho." He calls out to his partner: "Frank, hohohoho, we got another sucker with the "I'll be right back" rip off artist. "This is your first day on the job, right kid?

Cop: "You just flunked your on the job I Q test. Get another job kid. Ever think of getting into another line of work, like selling shoes for a living? However, sometimes serendipity happens and when it does, how sweet it is!

One Saturday in the wee small hours of the morning, a couple hours after all the bars had closed I encountered such a situation. I was sent to an apartment building on London Avenue, to pick up a lone middle aged woman who was on a mission to purchase some booze. Once she got into the taxi, she gave me an address to go to, telling me she was going there to pick up a case of 24 of beer. When we got to the bootlegger's door, I saw her squeeze two twenties out of her tight fitting slacks. I then I watched her walk around to the back door. Soon, she returned, struggling with the case of beer. When she neared my car, I hopped out and took the beer from her and put it in the trunk. I told her that, by law, we had to put the beer in the trunk, which she didn't object to. When I pulled up to the front doors of her apartment building the lady rolled out of the taxi and started walking away heading toward the apartment door. "Where are you going?" I screamed "you haven't paid me yet!" Smugly, she answered, "I already paid you." She then continued wavering toward her apartment building's front doors laughing to herself. It brought back memories of my first rip off experience in my early days of my initiation into cabbie career 101, when I got handily ripped off by a man using the same tactic, only this time I had collateral: her case of beer was in the trunk. This time I had the upper hand. Thank you God! I shouted with great exhilaration. From now on I'm going to attend church!! With great enthusiasm I simply called out to her and said, "Thanks for the free beer you left in my trunk! Goodbye!" I then drove away. Later that night I sold her case of beer to another thirsty beer drinker. I earned an easy forty bucks. Now I was the con but I didn't feel any guilt about it. I felt no remorse, she planned to rip me off but it backfired on her. I knew by the way she spun around on her heels that she realized that she had made a mistake. Now she was the one who was duped.

Sex and the Cabbie

*D*on't get too excited by the title. It is not my intention to write a smutty book about any graphically sexual escapades that I may have observed over the years while driving a taxi in the city of Winnipeg. That would be too easy to do and wouldn't require much talent on my part to achieve. I feel I would be abusing whatever talent my Heavenly Father may have given me, and thus, offend my God. I am a Christian but that does not mean I am a prude. I am not so naive so as to think we live in a perfect world or that I am oblivious to the carnal world of sex and depravity which goes on around us all, on a regular basis. Yes, I like you, do oftentimes become exposed to the carnal elements of our world but I will not inundate you with those sordid salacious details for the sake of providing you, the reader, with a mental thrill in order to entice you to buy this book. Following are a few sad stories that I experienced over the years have sexual connotations. With this basic rudimentary explanation, please read on.

129

Homosexuality: My older sister once asked me if 1 had ever been propositioned by a gay man. Remember this was in the 70's when homosexuality was still in the closet and never openly talked about. 1 said yes, many times, but 1 always tried not to be offensive or judgmental when turning down their offers. 1 can only say that homosexuality is not for me. 1 don't understand it, but 1 tear up at times when 1 see the devastating hurt, pain, and suffering, many people in the gay community are often inflicted with or subjected to. One time in a heated debate on the subject, a friend, asked me what 1 would do if my son or a close family member confided in me that they were gay. My answer was that 1 would just love him or her. Rod Stewart had a song out in the 1970's which told the story about a gay man who's father violently beat, disowned, then and ostracized him from the family. Consequently, he learned to live on the streets, leaving him exposed to the dangerous elements of the world, which eventually did him in. In the end the young man ended up a murder victim, with little concern by society. A few lines in the song said,

In these days of changing ways, so called liberated days a story comes to mind of a friend of mine.

Georgie boy was gay 1 guess, Nothing' more or nothing' less, the kindest guy 1 ever knew

His mother's tears fell in vain, the afternoon George tried to explain

That he needed love like all the rest.

Pa said there must be a mistake, How can my son not be straight, After all I've said and done for him.

The song, overall, struck a sad chord with me. I once read, a long time ago, though I can't remember where, when, or who said it........ *"man's inhumanity to man is only surpassed by man's inhumanity to animals"* Being abandoned, ostracized, from anyone's family is the ultimate pain for anyone to experience. I could never abandon my son if he were gay though I know I would feel very uncomfortable at times. I would rather suffer quietly in pain than to see my son live in anguish. Live and let live I say. Love everyone. That's what God taught us. There are no exceptions!

Dancers: During my years of driving a cab in the city of Winnipeg I often drove strippers from one bar to another. Either I was driving them to work, or from work, and sometimes, to private functions. While exotic dancers are a step up from hookers some incorporate that trade into their act but most don't. They don't need to. Exotic dancers are somewhat like celebrities in that they tour the country and solicit high profile bars via their personal resume to land a gig. They can earn three to five thousand tax free dollars a week. On top of that, the classier bars provide a safe house for them to live in while they are on contract. Also, their employers provide protection for the dancers at all times. The girls are taxied to and from the bars and they don't have a pimp to suck up most of their earnings. Nor are they around to get them addicted to drugs thus create a dependency that they can effectively use to exploit them easier. Unfortunately, like prostitutes, some do hooked on drugs and end up living miserable lives. I got to know many over the years and most were nice girls who had graduated from a life of prostitution to a life of dancing. No matter at what level one may transition into the sex trade; it is still a dangerous line of work to get into. I remember Gordy, one of our master dispatchers, would send me out to a certain bar to pick up a certain dancer. For example he would say, "Gay Cavalier for Frenchie, the boom boom girl." I chuckled when Gordy said that because it always elicited some off color comments from the other drivers who happened to be listening to their radios at the time.

I remember one dancer, whose name I will not mention, who was a beautiful shapely woman with long blond hair and deep blue eyes. I remember she was a prolific stripper in that she was always busy. I got the impression that she was in a frenzied state of mind in her bid to earn as much money as possible in order to achieve whatever financial goal she may have set for herself. She performed at bars in the morning. She did gigs in the afternoons, and, of course, in the evenings and late at night. But she did something most other dancers rarely did. She hired herself out for private functions such as stag parties, private trade functions and any other corporate entities that may have a reason to throw a bash for their brotherhood. I was amazed how busy she was because I drove her many many, times, to her gigs. What I remember most about her is that she had a beautiful angelic looking little girl. They lived way up Henderson Highway in an upscale high rise. The little girl was four years old and seemed very attached to her mother. Like her mother, she had long golden blond hair and deep, sparkling blue eyes. The girl sounded intelligent, as indicated by her advanced verbal exchange with her mom. Like I said she was beautiful. A more beautiful little girl there never was! It pained me every time her mom would drop her daughter off at a friend's place, on her way to the bar. I always got an ominous feeling in my gut every time I saw that little angel scoot out of my cab and into the waiting arms of strangers. I know the violent world sex workers face on a daily basis and I worried about what would happen to the daughter if her mom met a deadly fate, which happens often to sex trade workers. I sometimes brought the subject up with mom, but when I did, she got very defensive about it. Then she would get upset and storm out of my car. I had to learn to shut my mouth and remain impartial about it. This stripper was ambitious. She would never turn down a gig and I drove her to private engagements all over the city, even upscale

133

apartment buildings, some, not so upscale. Bad idea! Unfortunately, while performing at a private stag party somewhere in lower Fort Gary, she somehow ended up flipping over the balcony of a ten story building, where she fell to her death. I always questioned the real story behind that tragic incident. Was it an accident, or did someone toss her over the edge? The most pertinent question in my mind is what ever happened to that beautiful little girl. I remembered, in our heated discussions, when mom told me, there were no family members around and no close friends whom she would trust her little girl's future to, if something ever happened to her. Now, something had happened to her and now the vultures would come out. I was heart-broken about it. There wasn't anything I could do about it. If I had had the opportunity, my wife and I would have adopted that little girl! I can only hope she was rescued. That poor, beautiful, innocent, little angel was left to the predators of the world. I only hope God sent one of His angels to rescue her. It doesn't happen often enough. Hence, another innocent victim lost to the sex trade! The sad reality is that she probably followed into her mother's footsteps or worse, became a hooker or porn star. Now that's a real oxymoron, porn star. Could it be the same as happy hooker?

Not So Happy Hookers: I got to know a lot of prostitutes over the years and a more exploited group of people does not exist in this world. Of all the victims in our society, hookers are the most violently abused. Occasionally I would overhear people in my car talk about how wonderful it would be to works as a prostitute for a year or two then retire wealthy. My thoughts were, you have no idea what you're talking about. I learned that virtually all prostitutes were sexually exploited as young children, by their fathers or other close family members! What a way to start out in life! Many people think that being a hooker is a lucrative, profitable, and a somewhat glamorous, career choice. The reality is that, that life style is horrendously violent, non profitable and, more often than not, deadly. Martha Street which runs off Higgins Avenue was where a lot of hookers openly plied their trade. It was just near the fire hall only a few blocks away from the busier Main Street strip. Best of all, it provided a retreat from the cops, and anonymity, where Johns felt comfortable approaching the gals. The area was quiet and offered a sense of free un-obstructed activity. I was drawn to the place when I wanted a break. It was there that I would take the opportunity to read my bible. I parked across the street from the sexual activity taking place. I was intrigued but not interested in getting involved with hookers. I didn't want the hookers to think I was soliciting them so I stayed in my taxi. I knew what was going on but I went there anyway because I figured that they wouldn't bother with me, being a cabbie and all. Besides, I parked out of the way of the action. I was spunky in those days and I wasn't worried about the pimps of whom I felt no fear. Leave me alone and I'll leave you alone. I was wrong in the sense that hookers approached my cab, at first, to proposition me, but when they saw I wasn't interested, they would just sit in my cab looking for a place to rest, and then they would chat with me for a spell. It was always an interesting conversation if not enlightening. I remember this one prostitute whom had talked with me a few times, noticed my bible that I was holding in my hand and asked me, "Is what I'm doing wrong?" the question threw me off a bit. I figured she probably thought, because I was reading a bible, that I was judging her. I struggled for an answer. After a few stuttering words I said, "Yes, it's wrong according to the bible." I then quickly went on to say, "But I am not judging you! As a child of God, which you and I both are, it is not my job to judge you. You are just as important in the eyes of God as I am or anybody else and just because I have a bible it doesn't mean I am superior to you in any way!" She didn't say much after that and soon left. It wasn't my task to preach to hookers or anyone else, for that matter. I only spoke about gospel things, when they asked, or if they brought it up.

I remember this one sex worker who seemed a bit more civil than the others. We had spoken together a time or two. Early one morning, at the end of her shift, she asked me to drive her home. When I arrived at her apartment we chatted for a few minutes. She lamented a bit about her chaotic life. I quietly and as softly as I could speak said to her, "You don't belong here." It must have struck a chord because she went quiet, stared at me and said, "These are all my friends. I work with them every day. They're an important part of my life. I love my friends." I thought about that a minute and answered, "you will make new friends. You don't have to disown the friends you have now, just move on to greener pastures, so to speak!" A month or so later, she disappeared from the streets. I will never know if I helped her or not, I can only hope so.

In those days (early 70's) a working girl took in an average of $800 a night. I wondered why, if they were earning that much money, they were broke all the time? I remember watching an exhausted hooker standing on her street corner shivering uncontrollably, waiting to make one more score so she could have enough money to take a taxi home. She had already worked 12 hours, but her stash was spent. Where did the money go? To her pimp! To drugs! Prostitution is not a happy way of life. It's lewd, crude, and diabolical. I remember seeing a mother, age 28, waiting for a John. Her 14 year old daughter, stood beside her, waiting for her John as well. What a sad, self exploitive life!

Left For Dead: There was a dirt road that ran from Panet road, by the oil refinery, to Archibald, by which many cab drivers used frequently as a shortcut to get to downtown Portage Avenue. There were no street lights along that line so it's a dark, dreary, and muddy ride where mischief can happen. The road is well maintained in winter but in the spring, when the snow begins to melt it's a washboard. There are many pot holes to shake the beans out of your vehicle and where high muddy snow banks line either side of the road. If you take that route even once, it means that a quick run to a car wash is required. One night, while travelling down that road, one of our drivers spotted a woman of petite build lying atop this filthy mud covered snow-bank. She looked like a broken, discarded, doll left to die, probably by her john. It's a common well known fact, that often, when the john has done his business, he goes into a rage, and takes his guilt out on the hooker. Her $5000 white fur coat was covered with blood. She was barely alive. She had been stabbed seventeen times. The driver radioed the dispatcher to call the police. When the cops got to the scene, it had taken them so long that the driver had carried the hooker to his car and drove her to St. Boniface Hospital. Miraculously, she survived. The next day a couple of detectives from forensics showed up at the garage and spent hours processing the vehicle for evidence. I never heard if they ever caught the creep who tried to murder this woman, but I don't think they ever did. I guess that's another strike for hookers and prostitutes. This is another fact that being a hooker is not a glamorous life. When something happens to them, nobody cares! There is a lack of concern or a show of sympathy from society in general.

Night Sticks Versus Flashlights

I've seen cops in action a lot of times over the years and I have to say that most cops walking a beat have ice in their veins at times. I often saw cops attacked by groups of men and I noticed that some cops took necessary precautions to get as much of an edge as possible. I noticed for a time that some of the cops walking the beat on Main Street were carrying extra long flashlights that resembled, and served, as an improvised, night stick. One late evening I observed an officer walk into a greasy spoon coffee shop on Main Street. Right away I had a feeling of dark apprehension come over me. He walked in all alone and I noticed some seedy-looking characters eyeing him. Sure enough a biker looking dude started mouthing off to the cop and then stupidly gave the cop a violent push. The officer almost lost his balance which gave a couple observers sitting in close proximity to the spectacle the idea to get involved. Two men quickly moved out of their booth but before they could do anything serious, the officer swung the flashlight like a ninja warrior with great speed and dexterity. It crashed across the skull of the first biker sending him reeling against the counter and a second later, a second blow rendered the thug unconscious. Before the second biker reached the fracas the officer spun around and landed a vicious blow across his forehead, knocking him out cold too. The third biker instantly threw his hands up in the air and over his head as he fell to the floor in a self protective stance. The cop struck the third biker across the back of his head. This third biker didn't appear to be a threat to the cop but he suffered the same fate as the other two anyway. That flashlight caused a real mess as the place quickly became blood spattered. Instantly, cops started filling the place as a multitude of cops showed up and rushed in to help a fellow officer. I thought to myself, that cop doesn't need any help, but the dumb biker's sure do. In no time ambulances showed up and started hauling them away to the hospital. I don't know why the whole thing started in the first place but once moron number one started the ball rolling the cop quickly ended it and reinforcements quickly flooded the place.

Courtroom Humiliation

I once heard a commercial over the radio that said that two people die every day in Canada as a result of drunk drivers taking the wheel. That's reckless endangerment to say the least. I have no soft spot for drivers who drive while intoxicated but I did feel for this one gentleman who got charged under this law. He was of English extraction who owned a printing shop in the city. It was close to Christmas and he celebrated the occasion with his staff on a Friday afternoon. He wanted to show his appreciation to his employees and threw a party which not only included a festive buffet, but supplied a lavish array of alcoholic drinks. As alcohol inhibits our sense of judgment, so too did this printer find his judgment impaired. He saw no harm in driving after drinking alcohol, and decided to drive home. Unfortunately he got stopped by the police at a Ride Program, administered the breathalyzer test, arrested, and then charged under the law. When I met this businessman, though it was months later, he was still distraught about his experience. With a shaky voice filled with regret he related his experience with his charge. This man seemed like a perfect gentleman, responsible and law-abiding in every aspect of his life, a man who never broke the law until this incident. He lamented how he worried himself sick at having to go to court and face the judge. It kept him awake nights, weeks before his trial. He said he was embarrassed and never talked about it with anyone hoping to keep a low profile. He said that, by the time he got to court, he was a nervous wreck. He prayed that he wouldn't meet anyone he knew in the court room and hoped there wouldn't be many people there that day. But wouldn't you know it he lamented, the place was packed. It was standing room only. It just so happened that on that day, the court room was filled with high school students as observers to the proceedings. It was the perfect opportunity for the judge to make an example of him in front of all these young people. He told me how the judge literally yelled at him for twenty minutes, calling him derogatory names, well heard in this silent court room. He screamed my name interjecting adjectives like idiot, fool, asshole and attaching character assassinating words like, irresponsible, loser, self centered, heartless, and a blight to society, a man worthy of prison and so on. Based on his telling of his experience it would take a gun at his back to get him behind the wheel again, even if all he did was smell a beer cap at a party. God bless .08 but there are still too many people, even to this day, who haven't gotten the message yet. Perhaps we need more severe consequences for those who insist on breaking this law as what happened to this man.

Patience Pays Off

*I*n the wee hours of a Friday night a huge biker party was going on at an old two story house near the corner of Luxton and Main, near the Safeway grocery store. There had to be a hundred Hell's Angels bikers there with their choppers scattered helter skelter on their property. You could hear the heavy metal rock music blasting a block away, and you could also hear the roar of the biker crowd partying on. Occasionally you could hear the sound of a beer bottle smashing on the street or against a nearby house. The noise carried a long distance away. At the far corner of the Safeway parking lot, the long row of cop cars sat neatly parked parallel to each other, directly across from the house, facing the party. There was an ominous feeling in the air as those cops sat, waiting. Two officers occupied each vehicle. Every once in a while a biker would stagger out from the party, mount his chopper, then take off down the street. Immediately a cop car would break away from the fleet and go after the biker. After about four of them left the party, followed by a police car, I had to see for myself what was going down. This is what I witnessed. When the cop pulled over the chopper the two cops went into their routine. The same routine you or I experience when we get pulled over by a cop, only, in this case, with more aggression and intimidation. The roadside meeting went something like this:

Cop: "License insurance, registration, please"

Biker: complies Cop: "Blow into this device sir. We want to see how much you've had to drink tonight

Biker: grabs his crotch. "Blow this pig!"

At this point both cops jumped the biker. They wrestle him to the ground, landing a flurry of punches to his head until they subdue him. They soon manage to slip the cuffs on him. The two cops then literally dragged the biker to the cop car. The biker cursed and screamed a litany of derogatory profanities at the cops the entire way. Even with the biker cuffed and mobilized in the back seat of the cop car, the biker kept resisting and thrashing about the whole time. Once the Hell's Angels bad ass was in the back seat, the senior officer threw himself on top of the cuffed biker and landed a dozen or so blows to his head. The souped up chopper sat precariously abandoned at the curb as the first cop car drove away. The whole row of cop cars waited patiently for their next victim to emerge from the party. One by one they picked off the bikers as they emerged from the party. Some made a run for it and the cops pursued them at high speed. None surrendered peaceably. Some ended violently, especially when night sticks came into play. I was really impressed about how the cops played the scenario. If they had stormed the party it would have been so messy and innocent people could have been hurt, including the officers. Instead they waited patiently and picked them off one at a time. Boys will be boys, the saying goes, but it seems violence follows close behind.

Main Street Cowboy

*D*id you ever have a stressful day at work but some event occurred that lifted your spirits and put a smile on your face. Maybe a colleague won the office pool or perhaps someone in the office had a baby. It's a special thing when something nice happens, something delightful, something unexpected. After all, we all know, nice things don't happen often enough in our lives.

Late one Tuesday night around three in the morning, I witnessed such a thing. It wasn't anything earth moving or spectacular but it was something light-hearted yet simple, that made me smile. It was during a cold snap one winter when the temperature finally improved. It was evident by the fact that it began to snow, for we all know that when temperatures improve after a cold snap, it snows. The world looked like a snow globe as large flakes of snow filled the air and floated lazily to the earth. I was heading north on Main Street past the Occidental Hotel. The streets were almost deserted as the bars had closed hours ago. I caught sight of a tall lean man with a cowboy hat riding a sleek horse right in the middle of the street. There was virtually no traffic as this guy galloped his horse on the west side of the street. I pulled over to the curb for a better look at this spectacle. The rider saw me pull over so he accommodated me by crossing over the cement boulevard and headed toward me, putting him on the wrong side of the street and thus, in the wrong lane of traffic. Of the vehicles that were on the road, most of them seemed to enjoy the show as well as I did, for they honked their horns in approval. At this, the cowboy pulled hard on the reigns. His long legged horse raised himself up on his rear haunches, his front legs vigorously pawing the air as if he were waving to the onlookers. It was just like being at a real rodeo with a real rodeo star. The rider then took off his Stetson and waved it wildly over his head, giving an enthusiastic whoop as he did so. He then spurred on the steed as he quickly shot up Main Street, soon to disappear down the nearest side street. Never to be seen again! Who was that masked man you ask? I have no idea, but he left a flutter in my heart that made life a little brighter for one brief moment. Thank you masked man, whoever you were! (He wasn't really wearing a mask) but he was more exciting than the real Lone Ranger.

Alcoholic Apprentice

There are times that I have witnessed incidences that were completely inappropriate. Most of the time I mind my own business, but there are times when things have been taken too far, especially when it involves children. It is at this point that I choose to interfere. One such incident occurred deep into the night when I picked up a young couple from a party and drove them into St. Boniface. It was sometime in the middle of winter on a really cold night. I guessed the couple to be in their early to mid twenties. Mom and dad hopped into the back seat along with a baby dressed in a heavy snow suit. I guessed the baby to be a little less than a year old. Needless to say, it didn't surprise me that the baby was bundled up in thick winter clothing because of the weather. The dad handed me the sleeping child as he wedged himself into the back seat. Once there I handed the baby over to mom. It was then that I noticed that the child didn't move a muscle. The child hung like a limp rag draped over my arm. I said, "Look at that, your kid didn't move

149

a muscle. If I didn't know better, I would think he was drunk." Then I took the boy's arm, raised it up then let it go. It instantly fell to his side. In total amusement, his mom and dad burst into laughter and said, "He *is* drunk. We fed the little bugger beer until he passed out. That's why he won't wake up." I was horrified by such a shocking admission. "Why did you do that?" I asked in disbelief and awe. My jaw was still gaping open when the dad continued.

"We want the little guy to learn to hate the taste of beer" dad answered proudly; as if he had discovered the cure for alcoholism. "That's right added the mother. When he grows up we don't want him to ever drink a drop of booze in his whole life!" I couldn't believe what I was hearing. I thought, only Neanderthals thought like that. That poor kid, I thought, passed out in his parent's arms, lying there like a limp rag, oblivious to the world. I was incensed but yet upset about good intentioned ignorance on the part of the parents. I was at a loss for words as I thought long and hard before launching into a non-threatening offensive response. I knew they loved their kid but they were going about this all wrong. In the calmest voice I could muster I said, "I think your idea is really good. No mom or dad wants their kid to become a drunk and I think that's a good place to start. I think you need a better approach than getting your baby drunk. Getting your kid drunk like this will just have the opposite effect. Doing this, will condition your son to not only love booze, but to build up a tolerance for it. Feeding your baby beer until he passes out is not only dangerous but will put him on the express lane to alcoholism. There are agencies out there that will pick up on your ideas to help your kid stay away from alcohol and be aware of its dangers. The Children's Aid Society is just one example." It got really quiet in the cab so I figured they were thinking about their actions. I felt it was time to sound non-judgmental or patronizing so I decided to stop the preaching. "But you've got the right idea. Don't give up, stay on the right track and things will work out for you guys." For the rest of the ride, all was quiet. No one uttered a word. Once we arrived at their destination, I helped them out of the cab and shook their hands. I wasn't convinced that they understood the gravity of their actions. I worried that this conversation would vaporize in the morning and that they would take no action to curb the addictive avalanche they had set in motion in this young baby's life. I felt I had to do something. The potential repercussions were too great. Once I reached our destination and before I drove away, I wrote down the name and addresses of the people and reported them to the Children's Aid Society the following day. I don't know what followed with that family; I can only hope they never again would find humor in putting an innocent baby on the road to a life time of misery through addiction. This family needed help and I can only hope they got it in time.

Dumb Stunts

I remember the Evil Kenevil era when the stunt devil marveled the world with his motorcycle exploits by driving his speeding motorcycle over inordinate numbers of parked cars, trucks, and buses. It seemed that the world was convinced there was nothing Evil Kenevil couldn't fly over. It culminated when the stunt rider convinced the world that he was going to jump over the Grand Canyon. It turned out that that was really a con job. It would have been just as logical to say that he was going to leap from a cliff in Halifax and land his bike on the grounds of Normandy. Impossible in either case! But he manipulated the media enough through newspaper stories, television and radio broadcasts, that it was almost conceivable, though any sane person knew it was not. Evil drummed up enough hype that the press and networks showed up on the appointed day to watch Evil Kenevil attempt to jump the Grand Canyon. Even Evil Kenevil knew it was an impossible task and he attached a parachute to his back, so that, when he zoomed from the launch pad, he immediately opened his chute and waved good-by to his motorcycle and a big hello to the millions of dollars that amassed into his bank account thanks to the millions of people who viewed his stunt and bought the many millions of related trinkets such as plastic Evil Kenevil figures, lunch boxes, coloring books, pajamas, t-shits and everything imaginable to the greedy marketers. There was no risk to Evil Kenevil whatsoever. With the use of his parachute he eventually softly floated down to join his mangled bike on the canyon floor. Because of that crazy stunt, other daring people came up with dangerous stunts of their own, some of them fatal! I particularly remember watching an athletic young African American man perform a stunt on television that I thought made Evil Kenevil's stunts look like child's play in comparison. The first time I saw it, my heart sank into my chest and I let out a sharp gasp. It showed the young man standing on the centre line of a major highway with a car zooming toward him at eighty miles an hour. At the precise time the young man had mentally calculated, he ran toward the speeding vehicle and at the exact second that I expected him to be violently killed, the young man jumped as high as he could straight up and over the car as it flew underneath him. Lucky for that young man he survived, but many others who tried to copy that act weren't as lucky. Some found their calculations a bit off and when they landed a hundred yards or so away, they were dead. Some found out the hard way that they couldn't jump as high as they thought they could. I remember reading in the newspaper that this one fool almost cleared the roof of the vehicle but his leg caught the automobile's roof and the cameras caught the fact that his leg from the knee down twisted four times after it hit. It was a stupid stunt and no one made a dime from it though too many died trying.

A long while after that, when I thought the fascination with stunts had died down, I came upon a scene that told me that that wasn't the case. It happened late one evening. I had dropped off a couple at the apartment building near the corner of Munroe and London Avenue. There was a short stretch of paved road that ran half a block and ended at steel guard rails cutting off Munroe from newly constructed Concordia Road. There was a laneway that ran parallel with Munroe that began south of Munroe and ran all the way to Gateway Road. I had turned right on Munroe with the intention of parking my car for a few minutes in order to give me enough time to catch up on my trip sheet. The first thing I saw was an older teen standing in the middle of the road and a car zooming from the laneway on my right toward him. The teen attempted to jump but he failed miserably, landing with a loud crash on the hood of the other teen's junker. The vehicle came to a quick stop but the teen was in pain. It didn't take me long to realize what these two numbskulls were trying to do.

Shocked, I immediately hopped out of my cab and ran over to help the teen up. Luckily, no one was seriously hurt. I chastised him for trying to perform a stunt that no one attempted to perform anymore because too many people had died trying. They were smiling as I walked away but I think their failed attempt convinced them I was right.

The Un-Merry Christmas Party

*O*nly once in all my years at driving a cab did I work on Christmas Eve, and that was only after my wife and I had a dreadful falling out. However, I did drive almost every New Year's Eve for years. I found that was the most profitable day of the year to work, both in terms of bringing in a huge take and racking up tremendously large tips! If the weather was right, that is, not too cold, but relatively mild, the payday often turned out to be record breaking! Mild temperatures meant that the house parties lasted longer than usual and for some pleasant reason, which I can't fully explain, people were more civil.

On this one Christmas Eve around ten thirty, I was sent to a house party way up Henderson Highway. When I arrived there, the party was in full swing. It was a mild night and the place was lit up like a Christmas tree. I could hear the music blasting away full tilt with lots of

156

guys and gals socializing, or so I thought, in the plowed out yard and driveway. There was a full moon and the flood light illuminated the entire yard. My first concern with this call and all these party goers mingling about, was finding the person or persons who had called a cab. I stopped near the side of the house when a man flew around the corner of the building landing splayed out a few feet in front of my front bumper. The man's face was covered with blood caused, I figured, by a few punches thrown by whoever wanted the man taken away. The man was stinking drunk and from what I could conclude, was harassing too many guests at the party. He was babbling incoherently and he couldn't stand up without help. When the people saw my taxi, a few of them immediately came to my car and said, "Take this asshole away, he just wants to cause trouble! Get him out of here!" This sentiment was echoed by others, men and women alike. The man was a pathetic sight and by the looks of his bloody face and his babbling, I feared that his beating could end up more serious and maybe even fatal, if he didn't escape this scene. I spotted a man who was just in shirt sleeves with a look of anger on his face. I concluded that he was obviously the aggressor. I guessed that the blood covered victim was the antagonist. Leaving him here wasn't an option I felt comfortable with. The guy was drunk out of his mind, so I asked the man with the white shirt where I was suppose to take this guy. The host barked, "I don't care where you take him, just take him away." With that, he and a few others in the group, picked the guy up and flung him in the back seat of my cab. They then abruptly walked away, heading back around the corner of the house. It looked like they were intending to rejoin the party going on inside. I quickly hopped out of my car and yelled, "Whoa, whoa! Someone has to come with me to drop him off! The guy's covered in blood bleeding all over inside the car and he's so drunk I can't communicate with him. Which means I have no way of knowing where he's going and once I get to this mysterious place I can only hope I can get paid."

The host spun around and spat, "That's not my problem, man.!" And he walked on. I felt helpless watching the group walk away. "No way bud!" I shouted; "I'm going to call my dispatcher and report an emergency situation and to send police pronto." "The word, *emergency* will get them here in a hurry and I'm sure they'll be anxious to charge somebody with assault when they get here." The host started to protest but he stopped himself and, with his hands in the air. He and another man got into the car and we dropped the drunk off at one of their friend's place which seemed to appease everyone. They helped the evictee out of my car and disappeared into the house and when they came out, I drove the two of them back to the party. He threw me a fifty dollar bill and apologized for the aggravation. "Merry Christmas" was all I said as I drove out of the snow covered yard.

Quirks And Quarks

Moon Row

On the lighter side of life, some things I've experienced driving a cab in Winnipeg are indeed unique to Winnipeg and indeed unique to cab driving itself. My background is French. I was green and fresh out of high school when I started working but it was the interaction with the public and people in general that I sometimes found difficult. One morning I was dispatched to Cox's bakery at Johnson and Henderson Highway to pick up an elderly Ukrainian gentleman. He was a large man with two bags of groceries. When I asked him where he wanted to go he gave me a number on Munroe Avenue, but because of his accent I heard "Moon Row". I repeated what I heard and he excitedly answered "yeh, yeh, Moon Row!" I drove up Henderson Highway unsure if I was going in the right direction, I searched my mental map of the area trying to think where this street could be, but nothing was coming up. As I was nearing Munroe I repeatedly asked if it was Moon Row and he answered in the same strenuous voice, Yeh, Yeh, Moon Row!" Could the gentleman actually mean Munroe and not Moon Row I wondered, or was it a different street altogether. As I drove past Munroe the customer got super excited shouting, "Moon Row, Moon Row". I thought he was going to explode as he rocked violently back and forth. I quickly pulled over to the curb and shut off the meter. In the best English and in perfect diction I asked again, "Is it Munroe?" when he gave me the "Yeh, Yeh, "Moon Row" again. Without further adieu, I drove him home with no further duress.

Dangerous Habit

*O*n another trip, I picked up a family from the Safeway store on Henderson Highway and Kimberly. Off we went to Martin Avenue, east of Gateway Road with a trunk full of groceries. Dad sat in the front, mom two teen age girls and a 9 year old girl sat in the back. As I pulled up in front of their home I slowed down but, just before I came to a complete stop, the young girl opened her door and jumped out. I immediately slammed the brakes, coming to a complete stop. As it turned out, the rear tire was on top of her left foot. Dad rushed to his daughter and instructed me when to slowly move. That was when the mother said about her daughter, "She always does that!" After checking the girl out, we unloaded the groceries and I drove the family to the nearest hospital. Everything was okay, no injuries. Mom and dad repeated to me the daughter's habit of hopping out of the back seat before the car had a chance of coming to a complete stop. I told them that in the future, to make the driver aware of the girl's dangerous habit. I Told the parents that I wished I had been warned and I knew that others drivers would like to be made aware of this as well. I stressed that every taxi driver wanted to avoid any and all injuries to their customers. Otherwise, the next time she might have been seriously hurt. The parents agreed with what I said but I doubted they understood *how* serious, because they laughed it off.

Muddy Outline

*O*ne beautiful warm spring day in late May when the snow had finally melted away, I saw a neatly dressed man madly running along Watt Street trying to reach his bus stop before the speedy oncoming bus came. It was a bright sunny day with spring fever in the air. The warm air resulted in black mucky water leveled to the curb. In spite of his determination to out run Transit Tom, it was obvious that he wasn't going to make it. As the bus neared, the guy glanced over his shoulder and came to the same conclusion I did. The man quickly turned his back to the street and in spread eagle fashion clung to the white wall of the nearby house, as the wave of muddy water splashed way over his head. After a few seconds, he moved away from the wall, leaving a perfect dark outline of his body. I pulled over to the next curb and I laughed myself to tears. He saw me laughing hysterically but said nothing as he walked past my car. He simply mumbled a few words which I couldn't make out and gave me the finger.

Meter Phobia

*Y*ou would think that taxi fares are an exuberant expense to people because they freak out so easily at the cost displayed on the meter, this at a time when the meter started at fifty five cents and jumped ten cents. Heck, in the 1970's, when I drove cab in Winnipeg, you could take a cab from the far east end of Transcona and go all the way to the airport for about twelve bucks. It seemed people always wanted to make a big deal, hoping to beat the meter. On many occasions when a person would flag me down on the street he would instantly and anxiously urge me to *not* turn the meter on. "Don't turn the meter on!" they'd say while panting. I'm only going a few blocks away. Here's five bucks, keep it." In many instances I knew the fare wouldn't run over two bucks so I quickly stuffed the bill in my shirt and quickly dropped him or her off. So you could say I benefited from people's taxi phobia. I really savored the cash from these meter phobic individuals.

Fearful Description Aids Car Thief

*L*ate, one Saturday night, one of the company's drivers had his cab stolen by a gang of young native men somewhere deep in the north end. The dispatcher sent me to lend support to the rookie driver. When I got there the cops had been called but hadn't arrived on the scene yet. A large group of about a dozen young native men loitered near the street corner with a shaken and flustered driver among them. When I pulled up to the crowd the driver separated himself from the group and hopped in the front seat of my car. The crowd quickly gathered at my window. A self appointed spokesman blurted out that he saw the thief drive away with the taxi. When I asked him which way he went once he got to the corner, a chorus of voices said he turned right. I instantly took off after the stolen cab knowing the group was lying. When I got to the corner I turned the opposite direction that the crowd had directed. I turned left. There, just a short distance away, I spied the abandoned vehicle. It was idling and luckily no damaged had been done to the car.

I instructed the rookie to get into the stolen taxi and drive it back to the corner where most of the group still lingered. I told him I would join him there and together we would wait for the police to arrive. As it turned out the cops were there when we got back. The cop in charge asked the driver what happened and, for a description of the perpetrator. Without being asked, several members of the group said they saw the perp exchange sweaters with another man before he disappeared somewhere in the complex. I could tell by the mischievous mood of the group that they were trying to hatch a plan to throw off the investigation of the police. They didn't have to do much to accomplish their goal because the driver was so rattled by the whole incident that the description he gave to the cops was so off that, that alone ended all hope for the law to apprehend the proper thief. He described him as being about 5 feet tall with blond straight hair and blue eyes. The majority of the young men who lingered near the crime scene looked like a native senior high school basketball team. They all had black hair typical of their native heritage. I chuckled to myself because it made me think of the scene in the movie "The Russians are coming, The Russians are coming" when Brian Keith, the sheriff, asks the Russian sub captain what nationality they were. In a heavy Russian accent he answers, "Swede." This was close to the same. When it was determined I wasn't needed anymore, I suggested to the driver that he go home and relax. Then I left. So much for a reliable testimony I thought.

Accidents

*L*ike I said in my prologue at the front of this book I am from a small town in Northern Ontario, or as I often tell people, I'm a hick from the sticks. I had only been driving a few years and only in my small town in Northern Ontario. However, I felt pretty confident behind the wheel and I very much enjoyed driving my taxi. This one mild spring day on a Saturday afternoon, I was driving this nurse to work. She was employed at one of the three hospitals located down the end of Morley Avenue. I believe it was the Princess Elizabeth hospital.

I was driving along with my window mostly down, enjoying the warmth of the sun on my body and the cool breeze on my face. The snow was mostly gone and I was absorbing the radiant heat from the sun's rays heating the inside of my car. I had no traffic lights in front of me and as far as I could see it was clear sailing down Morley with nothing to stop or slow down for. When I was a little better than half way down Morley, I suddenly noticed a car approaching from my left. He was cruising along, enjoying the day much like I was. It didn't look like he was going to slow down and he was heading right for me. Since there were no stop signs in front of me, I assumed automatically that the driver coming from my left, had to have a stop sign in front of him and he would soon stop. Suddenly I realized he wasn't going to stop and we crashed into each other as soon as we entered the intersection. His right front bumper hit my left front bumper and we moved kitty corner through the wide intersection. It felt like we were connected by our bumpers. We quickly moved to the south east corner of the street and together, climbed halfway up a huge oak tree at that corner. I had never been in an accident before so it shook me up, but not enough to ignore the safety of my passenger. Right away I checked on my passenger in the back seat to make sure she wasn't injured. Then I checked with the driver of the other vehicle. I was greatly relieved that no one was hurt. I reported the accident to my dispatcher who called the police and a tow truck to drag my taxi back to the garage. But first I waited for the cops and when they arrived and we were all trying to figure out what had happened. I was informed that there were no stop signs at any of the intersections on Morley. I had never known there was such a thing as "uncontrolled intersections" I found it profoundly incredulous that a street in a large metropolitan city like Winnipeg, and a critical one at that, being so near to three hospitals, would remove all the stop signs. It was insane to me.

I was angry. "How stupid!," I screamed at the cop who was taking down the information at the time. "I would expect that from my little teeny town to be somewhat a bit different like that, but not here with a population of half a million people!" The cop didn't engage me in the conversation but said that for all intents and purposes, I should be glad because I was in the right. In other words, the driver who plowed into me was in the wrong because he was supposed to yield to me because I was to his right. Of course in an uncontrolled intersection you must yield to the right of way. Apparently, the same applies in parking lots at shopping malls.

Needless to say, the accident ruined my day, but I did learn about uncontrolled intersections, plus, this time, nobody suffered any injuries. The nurse just left the scene and made her way to work a few blocks down on foot. She didn't pay me and I didn't ask. When the tow truck finally showed up, I rode back to the garage with the tow truck operator then continued home for the evening.

Near Fatal Water Slide

I love Lockport. This is a small town a few miles north of Winnipeg. The name comes from the fact that they have locks to help the boats navigate their way up river. I love to watch the locks open and close as boats come and go throughout the day. I also love to watch the pelicans dive in and out of the water as they scoop up their dinner. They are so agile when they maneuver about the locks. I also enjoy tossing a Frisbee about with my friends or even just enjoying a burger inside the adjacent grille. Sometimes I enjoyed lying on a blanket reading a book under a shady tree nearby. All in all, Lockport is one of my favorite places to visit. Later they built water slides nearby, and I spent many sunny days enjoying the facility. When my kids got old enough I would take them to the water slides and we would make a day out of it with picnic lunches and all. As a family we have stored up a lot of happy memories there.

I was happy when they built water slides at Lockport until I saw a near fatal event take place that scared the beans out of me. I was standing nearby watching the kid's wiz down the slide screaming and wailing like banshee warriors, like all kids should do at the amusement slides. I noticed that at one curve along the way kids were catapulted vigorously, and I thought dangerously, close to the fence. On the other side of that fence was an electric power station. I remember fearing that a kid might be in danger of being tossed over the fence and into the fenced in electric power grid. Just as I thought it, it happened. A skinny kid about ten years old shot out over the steel fence and landed inside the grid. He immediately stood up as if he had performed a daring death defying feat. He had, but he was totally unaware of it. The kid threw up his arms in victory, savoring the moment, then immediately jumped back onto the water slide and continued his ride down to the pool area. The adults who had seen the spectacle gasped loudly and I heard then say that the slide was built too close to the electrical compound. I heard one of them say as they marched to look for a person in authority to report this to. "Some kids going to get fried if they don't secure this ride, and I mean now! I moved away that same year but I hope no kid, or adult for that matter, fried as some feared might happen. In spite of the beauty of Lockport I remember reading in the paper that a kid fell into one of the locks as it was being filled with water. Naturally, his father jumped in to rescue his son. Unfortunately both father and son drowned. When I visited the place a few years ago I noticed that there were no rescue items available to use in case such a tragedy were to happen today. No life jackets, no ropes or alarms, no activating device to sound the alarm in case someone needed rescuing. I'm surprised no one has brought that to the attention of the ground authorities yet. I guess once someone dies and a huge lawsuit follows; things will then change. Come on people, the place is too beautiful to ignore any longer.

Child Fatality

*E*motions run high when a child is killed, especially when the death is caused by a young driver recklessly racing up and down residential neighborhood streets.

One evening, I picked up a young mother who had experienced just such a tragedy. She lived in the London Street area of East Elmwood. During our conversation it came out that she was going out to attend a grief counseling meeting. This well dressed professional looking woman, who looked to be in her hid thirties, told me that her six year old daughter was hit and killed by a young driver a few years ago. The driver had had a few drinks and was racing with his buddy down their street. In this instance, the young inexperienced driver sped around at extremely high speeds with flagrant disregard for the safety of anyone. These two friends, numbed with alcohol, raced against one another for no rational reason other than for the pure joy of speed. In doing so, they drove recklessly and in this case, fatally, striking this young girl. She said her little girl had been playing tag with her friends, enjoying themselves. As often happens with young children, they tend to get overexcited and forget all about safety, and borders get forgotten. The mother wiped away tears as she said, "Sherrie ran out onto the street from between two parked cars. I could feel this mother's pain and so I stopped talking. I wanted to give her an opportunity to lead the conversation. I wanted to change the subject so I remained in silent. After a minute she continued speaking on the subject. I guessed that she replayed this story many times in the past and I thought that allowing her to continue, may have been therapeutic. I told her that I was very sorry for her loss. Even though I was married at the time, we had no children. I told her I would never be able to get over something as traumatic as losing a child. When a pause came I asked her, "When did this happen?"

"Three and a half years ago!" she answered. I asked what the charges were for the driver. She told me he only had to pay a fine and lost his license for a determined amount of time. I said "Where is the justice in that"? I asked how she and her husband managed to get over this tragedy. She told me that she and her husband were devastated about it for a long time. They went together to a grief therapist for treatment. Then they joined a grief counseling group with people who had experienced similar devastating tragedies. These were people who met on a regular basis. They were people who had lost children in similar fashion. In the lull of the conversation I thought to myself, I hope they sued the jerk! It was as if she heard my thoughts when she said, "My husband and I consulted a lawyer and we sued him over and over again. My husband was never satisfied with the results of the settlement. He wanted to break the guy until he would become literally, financially destroyed, with nothing left to his name. He was filled with so much hate that it got to a point where I couldn't take it anymore. Even if the kid was a billionaire and he was liquidated of all his assets, we could never have our child back? NO!! Nothing we could do was going to bring our little girl back. We had to find another outlet for our grief.

As a desperate measure for closure, the therapist suggested that they invite the young man who drove the car that killed their daughter into their home for dinner. He felt it would help both parties understand each other better and help the grief process to take effect. She told me that they decided to try that, even though her husband was still so angry at *the punk who had murdered his little girl* as she put it.

She told me that the young man expressed deep sorrow and regret for what he had caused and asked through tears, for forgiveness. He said that since the accident he hadn't driven. He admitted his fault and cried genuine tears of compassion in front of them. At the height of his dinner, the young man pulled out his wallet which showed them that he had no license. He

176

said he ripped up his license right after the accident. He told himself that he didn't deserve to have one. On close inspection of his wallet, this mother said, "I didn't see a license in his wallet. What I did see was a picture of my daughter set where his license would be. He still had her picture in his wallet!"

She told me that her husband, even after the visit, could never forgive the young man and continued to sue him until it was more than the mother could bear!

Eventually, their marriage broke up, ending in divorce. Her husband accused her of not caring about their daughter because she didn't want to go to court any more to sue her daughter's murderer.

When I arrived at her destination I was too choked up to speak. All I managed to squeak out was, "God bless you, mom!"

'Thank you" was all she said as she closed the door and walked away into the night. I wiped away my tears as I drove away.

Light Hearted Humor

I often remember odd incidences that I experienced over time, some of which are comical, while others are simply amusing, like the time I was driving a business man to the airport one early evening. I was stopped at a red light on Logan Avenue and Salter. The light turned green but I was lost in a daydream so I didn't move. After a few minutes, my passenger in the back seat, gently placed his hand on my shoulder, and in a soft gentle voice whispered, "Are you waiting for a lighter shade of green?"

Fly Window Invasion

*O*ne evening I was driving a woman home from her place of employment out in St James, to her home in North Kildonan. She shared an incident that happened to her one evening as she drove home from work. She was employed at a battery factory and her shift ended at twelve thirty a.m. The woman had to drive home alone, to her residence on Rothesay. This woman was paranoid to begin with, especially when it came to interacting with natives. She was just one of these women who feared natives, which explained why she locked all her doors when she left the factory. One Friday night saw her stopped at the red light at Logan and Main. She faced the approach to the Disraeli Freeway and she was sweating and hyperventilating, sitting there, white knuckling the steering wheel. Remember, this was Friday night and the woman was at the nucleus of native pandemonium. This was where fights and stabbings proliferated. She was telling me that her heart was pounding a mile a minute, waiting for the light to change. Her eyes stayed fixated on the lights, scared to death to look right or left. Older cars used to have a small triangular window called a fly window in the front door to allow fresh air to come in while driving. Suddenly the lady noticed a man's hand slowly moving into the car through this fly window, moving toward the lock button in her door. She said, "When I saw this creepy hand in my car, I panicked. I let out a blood curdling scream and stomped on the gas pedal. I shut my eyes tight and flew through the red light in a panic, anxious to get away!" She told me that she sped all the way home, and then she told her husband what happened. "He just laughed it off!" she said. The next morning a cop knocked on her door. The officer asked her if had had an accident at Logan and Main as she drove home last night. "Not really," the woman said. She continued to explain to the officer her recollection of the incident. "This guy tried to steal my car last night as I waited for a light at Logan and Main! However, I managed to escape. I stomped on the gas and flew through the intersection, barely managing to avoid an accident judging by the sound of screeching brakes around me. The cop smiled mischievously and answered, "The man who was trying to get into your car, gave us your plate number," With a twinkle in his eye he said, "He accused you of taking something of his as you drove away!" The woman said she loudly protested calling the intruder a liar! "Let's check this out," said the officer as he made his way to her parked car in the driveway. The cop opened the driver's door and reached inside and said, "I think this is what you stole from your native friend last night. He then pulled out the man's thumb that had been severed off and was still wedged in her fly window." She must have brought it with her as she sped away. He pulled out what looked like a baggy, and dropped the thumb into it. "I need to take this souvenir to the hospital, "the cop chuckled. "The man wants it back for reattachment" he said with a smile. The officer was laughing as he drove away, shaking his head in wonder. She said she was horrified at the sight she had seen. She said she was going to traded in her vehicle in for one with no fly windows.

Wild Women

*O*nce in a while fares can get hostile and sometimes fights can break out but I found it best to avoid confrontation altogether. I found that it was best to be aware of who I pick up, and how many people I pick up at any one time. On this one mid-week night, I picked up six young aboriginal women at a bar on Main Street and drove them to a high rise on York, not far from Broadway Avenue. I wasn't worried about this loud rowdy group, because they were all women and I thought I could easily handle them if I needed to. (I admit I was somewhat sexist back then and boy was I wrong) Besides that, they had purchased a twenty four pack of beer at the bar, which I insisted had to be put in the trunk. That, I felt, was my insurance for getting paid. We drove to the high rise building and I waited for one of the women to go inside to make sure that it was the correct location where the party was supposed to take place. This was my first red flag. Suddenly, there was silence in my car as everyone sat quietly awaiting the return of the scout. No one spoke a word until the lady returned. She cheerfully announced that it was the place where they needed to be, and all the women stepped out of the car. No one made a move to pay me. They were anxious to get the beer out of my trunk but they fell silent again when I announced the price of the fare as indicated on my meter. We all stood about for a few minutes then I said "well I can't open the trunk to get you your beer until someone pays me." No one moved so I got back into the car. They all got back into the taxi too and things remained quiet. I sat for about ten minutes when I announced I had to get paid immediately or I had to leave with their beer. The gal who had scouted the building gave a sigh and said she would look after the fare. I figured she had to have money, since she was the one who bought the beer. I gave myself a silent pat on the back, thinking I had gained victory over this group of women. I was over confident as I got out of my seat and walked to the back of my car to pop open the trunk. I reached inside and pulled out the case of beer. It was then that the entire group rushed me and attempted to wrestle the case of beer out of my arms. I knew immediately that I was beat. I did the only thing I could do under these circumstances. Since I knew that I was beat for the fare I wanted to score even a tiny bit of victory or a wee bit of satisfaction out of this situation. With as much force and strength as I could muster I threw the case of beer as high above and as far away over everyone's head as possible, which I figured had to be about twenty feet. It crashed loudly on the sidewalk a short distance away from the mob. The case of beer instantly exploded on impact with the cement sidewalk. The entire case of beer became enveloped in thick foam. It was as if a giant ENO pill had dropped into a large container of cola. Only ENO or like substance, could react so violently as it did to create such a result. The group rushed the foaming box of beer, hoping to salvage as much of the brew as they possibly could. I never did know how many bottles were destroyed, but, judging by the noise of many beer bottles breaking and the massive amount of white foam that escaped from the box, it was obvious to me that the damage was substantial. As the women concentrated on the broken box of beer I quickly got back into my cab and sped off leaving the women lamenting their loss. It was a bittersweet victory. Yes, I I lost the price of the fare but I did gain a 45% commission in wages. So, in that sense, I lost money, but I gained a hard earned lesson. I should not have opened the trunk until I got paid. I did salvage a great degree of satisfaction because all six women were grieving when I drove away. Their loss was more devastating for them than mine was for me.

Cabbie Humor

I think that due to the nature of the job, there exists a higher level of sensitivity among cabbies when good natured jocularity takes place. Listening to their reactions can be entertaining. At that time our number one driver in the fleet was a man called Jerry and every one called him Jervis. As it turned out he had suffered a nervous breakdown which caused him to be off work for some time. I was new at that time but I knew of his medical status. Some referred to him as nervous Jervis because he was high strung most of the time. It was about four in the morning and I was milling about with a few other drivers in the office waiting for the calls to start pouring in. The first call of the morning was from one of our regular daily customers. This oriental man owned a restaurant on Main Street near city hall and he had slept in that morning and was in a panic. The dispatcher who was among us in the office, turned to Jervis and simply said, Jervis go pick up so and so and take him to work. Jervis calmly nodded his head and sauntered out to his cab. Before Jervis got off the lot, the same customer called again wanting to know where his car was. The dispatcher told Jervis that the caller had called and asked where his car was and he told him the car was on the way and since he was only a few blocks away he would arrive in less than five minutes. Before the driver even got to the lights at Nairn, a block away from the office the customer called again. All of us drivers howled with laughter at the caller but we laughed even louder when the dispatcher relayed the call to Jervis who, in a rage, barked back, "You're kidding!" The absurdity became even more ridiculous when that same oriental gentleman called again before a Jervis could get to his home. The highlight reached its climax when Jervis announced that he had picked up his fare and was on the way to the man's place of business. The dispatcher said, "Good work Jervis, but please apologize for the delay!!" The office exploded in laughter, the roar of which could be heard out in the parking lot. One driver fell off the couch holding his sides as he rolled around on the floor. "No way!" was his only reply.

Ditzy Dangerous Dispatcher

There are codes the taxi industry uses which are essential for the daily operation of the business itself plus the smooth flow of communication between the drivers and the office. All this to ensure maximum efficiency and safety at all times. They are as follows:

10-1	repeat message
10-2	out for a quick coffee
10-4	message received ok
10-5	out for lunch
10-6	finished for the day
10-7	police assistance needed—emergency
10-8	street fare acquired
10-11	no fare

Depending on the communication skills of the drivers and the dispatcher, conversation between the two can be cut to a bare minimum thus eliminating unnecessary annoying chatter, which can give anyone migraine headaches.

Perhaps the most important code available to ensure driver safety is the 10-7 code when a driver may require emergency assistance. If the driver were to say to the dispatcher that he needed the police it could set off the passenger and put the driver life at risk. By using code it eliminates the risk the passenger might exhibit.

I have noticed in recent years some cabs possessed a large yellow light attached to the trunk of certain taxis with an adjoining notice that says, if this light is flashing, contact police immediately! Such drivers have access to a hidden switch that the driver is able to secretly activate when he feels threatened or fears for his life. Such circumstances sometimes occur during a drivers shift. Getting help quickly, when under such diverse circumstances is crucial. As a taxi driver, especially one who drives nights, you do sometime end up needing rescue from dangerous people in your car. That can take in the entire gamut of dysfunctional personalities of the whole human race. People on the run from the law; People escaped from prison; Sociopaths; Psychopaths; Murderers; Rapists; Serial killers; And, any other imaginable or unimaginable sick personalities the human race can churn out. While it is rare, it is possible a driver, male or female, could have such a personality in their car. Every once in a while, you hear about a driver being raped, robbed, stabbed, or murdered. I know it's unusual but once is too much. When this happens, it's vitally important to have that open field of easy flowing communication skills.

One extra crazy Friday night, (EVERY FRIDAY NIGHT WAS CRAZY) one of our drivers had four rowdy wild men in their cab. They were arguing amongst themselves whether or not they should rob the driver and steal his car. The lead moron who seemed like a career criminal, wanted to rob the driver, tie him up and dump his body on some deserted back road. Another one of the foursome thought it would be more logical to kill the driver straight out and eliminate the witness. Another of the group who turned out to be the most sane one, argued vehemently to forget the idea altogether. This car did not have an emergency light on the back. So, as best he could, when a small opportunity opened up, the driver relayed the 10-7 code to the dispatcher; relieved that he had managed to get the message out. This ditzy, moronic dispatcher blasted back to the driver, "WHAT DO WANT THE COPS FOR?!" This had an immediate reaction from the group, especially from the one who was all for the plot. He immediately had a switch blade at the driver's throat in a matter of seconds. Luckily, for the driver, the other three men acted quickly and overpowered the knife yielding thug and thrashed their way out of the taxi. The driver was pretty shaken up as he drove to the office. He was still shaking when he pulled up to the garage door, twenty minutes later. The driver pounced out of the taxi and sprinted to the office door, past the office lobby then stormed into the dispatch office. When the dispatcher turned to face the enraged driver, the driver viciously attacked him. Unfortunately, for the dispatcher, there were no drivers in the office to restrain the enraged driver. As it turned out, the dispatcher ended up with a severe beating but when the story came out, as to why it happened, no one felt pity for him; even Chuck. Thankfully the dispatcher quit two days later.

What city are YOU living in?

O ver the course of twenty two years as a Winnipeg cab driver, I drove through a few dozen blizzards. It always amazed me that people think that taxis are invincible and not impeded by the elements of nature, no matter how severe those elements of nature can become. I remember driving late one night during this horrendous blizzard where the snow was four to five feet high in the middle of the street. On this particular stormy night a woman in Transcona phoned for a taxi. The dispatcher explained it would be about an hour or so for a cab. She complained about the wait time but my dispatcher explained about the blizzard that was raging throughout the city. He also explained that he had only 4 drivers left from the entire fleet on the road, who were still out there, trudging along under horrible conditions. He went on to explain that the buses had long stopped running and most of the other taxi companies had closed up shop entirely. She relented somewhat of her unreasonable demands but she agreed begrudgingly, that she would wait for the cab no matter how long it would take. The dispatcher, thinking that this woman got the message, listened incredulously to the woman's absurd request. She asked that the driver come down the back lane so she wouldn't have to walk to the street to reach her cab. She wanted to avoid getting snow in her boots. In exasperation the dispatcher summarized what was going to go down. He said "Listen carefully Ma'am, I will get the driver as close to your front door as possible. When he gets there he will toot his horn. Once, and once only, if you are not out the door immediately, he will leave and I will not send another taxi, so I suggest you keep your eyes trained outside your front window. We do not have Sherman tanks or snow mobiles to use as cabs, which are what we would need to go down a back lane in this weather. We are operating under extreme emergency conditions, he explained as calmly as possible. We are doing our best!' With that he terminated the call, irritated by the callers' impracticality. And guess who was driving to get to this call? Me!

At this time I was driving mostly in the middle of the street following in snow packed ruts. The snow, in some places along the sides was reaching the edge of the widows. I pulled up in front of her house and leaned on the horn. The outside lights flickered on and off as a signal that she knew I was there. I was relieved and I wrote her address down on my trip sheet. Then, I relaxed, as I waited for the lady to appear outside. I concentrated all my attention on her front door. Finally, I saw her scurry out in a huff. As she got into the car there was a tirade of complaints. What kind of business are you guys running here anyways? Do you know how long I have been waiting for a taxi?? Also, I had to come out the front door wading through all this snow!! This is the last time I will be taking a taxi from this company. I just stared at her with a dumbfounded look on my face and gasped, "What city are you living in!? Does that white stuff out there look like dandruff? Next time, do me a favor, call Duffy's or Unicity, don't call us."

Creep Capitalizes On Storm

Usually, during a storm, homeless people stay in shelters and so on. A few cretins see this as an opportunity to prey on vulnerable people.

On another call, the second the fare got outside her front door she let out a blood curdling scream and moved into high gear as if she were being pursued by an axe murderer. She screamed all the way to my cab. She was still screaming as she threw herself into the front seat. She yelled at me to drive! She was hysterical. The look of horror was etched on her face and she kept looking back over her shoulder, to the trail she had just blazed from her front door. I could only stare in confusion looking for the cause of her terror, but I saw no evidence of anything alarming. I only saw deep footprints in the snow and the half opened front door of her home. In deep panic she shouted "GO!" I tried to object, "But maam your front door" She cut me off and shouted, "Drive, Drive! Drive!" all the while, flailing about with her door locked. Her whole body was in spasm. I shook my head in confusion, studying her face for an explanation as I quickly drove away.

After a few minutes the woman began to regain her composure enough to speak in a shaky voice. She told me that as she passed through her front porch and had opened the front door to step outside, she heard a man's husky voice ask, "Where are *you* going?" That was when she let out a scream and rushed out to my cab. "Who knows how long that man was in my porch?" she asked incredulously. "The hairs on my neck are standing up on end," she said. Mine are too I thought as I stepped on the gas. Who knows what this creep had in mind? I was only glad that she got out in time to meet me or she likely would have had her question answered. And that can't be good! I dropped her off at her friend's and instructed her to call 911. I can only assume that she did.

Annie

The most charismatic taxi driver and the one I admired and respected the most was a gal I nicknamed Annie (as in Annie Oakley). She also, exclusively, worked the evening shift, mostly cruising along the highest crime strips of all Winnipeg. She cruised the areas in, and around, Main Street, the area where most male drivers were too intimidated to cruise. She knew how to take care of herself. Her work ethic saw her consistently being in the top three highest earners. A hard working farm girl, she was built like a linebacker, only she wore a pony tail and a bomber jacket. I was fascinated by the way she went about conducting her taxi business. And she did so with honesty and integrity. It wasn't unusual in those days, to see a man or woman passed out on the sidewalk in front of any one of the many bars along Main Street. I often wondered whenever I spied someone passed out on the sidewalk, whether the person was dead or alive. I chose to never find out. I simply stayed away, avoiding the scene altogether. Not Annie. Whenever she spied an unconscious man or woman splayed flat out on the sidewalk, she would, without hesitation, quickly steer her cab to the curb like a hillbilly staking their claim to warm road kill. She was excited for her good fortune having stumbled across a 10-8 a taxi code for a street fare or someone who flags down a cab. Annie would quickly get out of her car and cautiously approach the man like a hungry wolf sniffing out the carcass of a dead moose.

She would lean in close and shout, "Where do you live?" or "do you have any money?" The lethargic response resulted in further prodding from Annie, all the while, raising her voice louder and louder. She would repeatedly boot the man in the pants as an attempt to revive him. The kicks weren't meant to hurt but to resuscitate. It sounded like an athlete kicking his duffle bag. The only sound I could hear from Annie's kicking was a dull moan. Often, there was no response at all. It was like trying to revive a mannequin but they were breathing. If the guy never regained consciousness Annie would move on to faze two of her routine. She would kneel down and roll the guy over on his side and dig out his wallet. She would then search through his wallet to discover where he lived, and how much money he had on him. With this found knowledge, Annie could quite accurately estimate the cost to drive the guy home. She would then extract the exact amount of money to cover his fare, and then she would put all the rest of the money back. Finally, Annie would slide the drunk's wallet back into his pants pocket.

With the destination known and the adequate amount of money in hand, it was time to continue.

Annie would open the rear side door of her cab, then she would grab the unconscious fare by the scruff of their neck and prop them up in the entrance of her taxi. There they stayed, sitting with their heads bowed, like a corpse. Annie would quickly scoot around to the other side of her taxi and open the other rear side door. With a few strainfull moves, she would launch herself into the cab far enough to grab the guy by the back of his neck, and haul him fully inside the vehicle. After making sure that all the doors were shut and the passenger safely inside, she would deliver him or her, home. As soon as the delivery was complete, Annie quickly returned to the streets, looking for another 10-8.

Another popular strategy Annie often employed to land fares was just as challenging. When there were no unconscious bodies to pluck off the city streets, she would walk into the *most* crowded and wildest bar on Main Street, (they were all wild, crowded, and violent). The bar tenders knew her on sight and knew her routine. They respected her because they knew that Annie never ripped a penny off any of them while they were at their most vulnerable. Besides, she was doing the bar and its patrons a valuable service by taking the most undesirables home. She would call out "Hey Charley, anybody you need taken out of here?" The bartender would point to some man passed out in his seat at a table and she basically went through the same routine as she did when these guys were on the sidewalk. Sometimes, the bartenders helped Annie by going through their pockets to extract the right amount of cash to cover their fares. Quite often the bartenders knew where these unconscious people lived so that sped things along nicely. Once taken out of the bar and on route home, everyone breathed a happy sigh of relief. Annie continued her marathon relay for hours and hours not going home until the sun rose on the horizon.

Chuck, the owner, the toughest, meanest, most ornery man I ever met in my life, was in the office early one morning having coffee and chatting with the boys. Chuck usually came in around 4 am but he didn't usually hang around for any length of time so this was a rare occasion. He was known for punching out drivers who got into accidents or for stealing fares, but he didn't make it a habit to socialize with them.

The conversation somehow got around to Annie when the dispatcher asked Chuck if he heard that Annie was robbed at gunpoint. Instantly, Chuck jumped out of his chair as if someone had burned him with a cigarette. He inhaled sharply and in feigned fear, eyes popping out of his head, exclaimed loudly, "I wouldn't do that!!!" This, coming from the same man who busted into an apartment where 5 men had run out on a driver without paying, and mopped up the floor with all of them then walked out with all their cash in hand. Everyone roared with laughter. And that summarized Annie.

Granny's Revenge

I remember a retired hay farmer and her son, also retired, who called a cab several times a week to do all sorts of running around. They used us to drive them to pay their bills, do their banking, and collect their groceries. We also drove them to their doctor appointments as well as to dentist visits. At first I didn't sense anything out of whack with them though they struck me as a bit odd. I guessed the son to be in his late sixties and mom to be in her mid eighties. They still lived on the family farm. I sensed mother had a touch of dementia though she was mostly functional. They were very nice people though I began to notice disturbing characteristics about them.

The son seemed to be a simpleton because he delighted in repeating my name many times during our conversations while driving in the taxi. Besides greeting me by my first name when he entered the vehicle, each sentence he spoke ended with my name. if I said, "it's pretty warm today." He would answer," "Yes Emile, it is Emile."

If I said "Going to visit the doctor today?" He would answer, "Yes Emile mothers not feeling well, EMILE, she's got a touch of flu" no matter how mundane the conversation, he used my name many times during the ride. It was as if he were proud for being able to remember it.

His mother wore a heavy pair of black wool pants which were noticeably discolored with urine, which soon made the whole car reek. The air inside the car was stiffing to the point that I found myself holding my breath for as long as possible. One morning I picked up the mother and son at their farm house but when they got into my cab, the smell of urine that morning was especially strong, probably because mom sat in the front seat this time. I could actually see the green pee stains visibly dyed into her clothing. The stench was so overwhelming that I rolled my window down, even though it was a chilly morning. The duo complained vehemently but I refused to roll it up again, feeling justified in doing so. When they coaxed me to comply with their request I steadfastly said no. I am never rude to my customers but this morning it was too much. I simply said, "The smell of pee is making me sick and your mother should have the good sense to wear freshly laundered clothes and take a bath as well, before going out in public. The conversation ended there and all conversation ceased for the entire ride, which ran half an hour. When I returned them back home and pulled into their driveway, feeling victorious in taking a stand and feeling I had gotten the message through to the old woman. The feeling of victory was short lived, because, when mom got out of my taxi and shortly after I had driven away, I noticed a formidable puddle of urine on the seat where mom had sat. I could see the look of victory on her face as *she* left the cab. The old woman had the last word and won her argument which was, up yours, driver! All I could do was drive back to the garage and clean up the mess.

Caught In the Act

*I*t is not my intention to expel tales of salacious events that people sometimes find themselves intertwined in. Although I have witnessed many unsavory human events in my travels I do not wish to enhance or sensationalize them. Most of all, I don't wish to smear the victims further or the perpetrators who commit them. I only wish to show that people make mistakes but there is always a way back if we try hard enough. Also, to shout "beware" of those who feign concern for victims who find themselves in the role of the sexually exploited? It could very well be that these supposed empathizers are really only motivated to capitalized on a victim's pain. They want to score a sexual victory for themselves by pretending to be your empathetic ally. They don't care that succumbing to your feelings of perceived justified revenge which only adds to victim's abuse, pain, and further feelings of exploitation.

One late fall Sunday afternoon, of all days, I got a trip somewhere in the 900 block of Talbot Avenue. A distressed middle aged couple got into the back seat of my taxi and told me to take them to the Gay Cavalier Hotel on Panet Road. Their intention was to pick up a couple cases of beer and then bring them back to the house again. The woman was stressed to the max as indicated by her flushed, teary face. I could tell she had been crying for a while. She was obviously heart-broken, the rage was self evident by her demeanor; swollen eyes, and flushed complexion. The man who accompanied her was not her husband, though the husband was the cause of all her grief. The man with her in the cab, I labeled, the instigator, but in reality a predator would have been a more appropriate label. He expressed disgust at her husband's actions. She caught him in a very intimate act of sex with her best friend. The instigator was very vocal, egging her on as they rode in the taxi. Without me asking, he loudly volunteered to disclose what had happened. "She caught her husband and her best friend engaged in oral sex!" he proclaimed. He then graphically described the event saying, "There he was like a crazed sex demon, just going to town on her!" He wasn't looking at the woman's face as he spoke "What's good for the goose is good for gander!" He then went back to what had happened being more graphic with each retelling of it. It was obvious to me his only role here was to influence the woman by stoking her fury and get her to feel justified into having sex with him, indifferent to the feelings of this poor woman who had just gotten her heart broken

204

and her life left in ruins. She said next to nothing the whole time. The whole time she just stared down at the floor or out the window at nothing. Occasionally, I could hear deep sobs of mourning from the woman curled up in the back seat, next to this predator. I didn't know what to say to her, so, when I was back at their house I stopped the cab as the man fumbled for his money. I said, "My professor at the university told our class that when things like this happen, the best reaction is to do nothing until it passes. He said never react when your under stress or in a fit of rage, because it's likely, whatever course of action you take, will be the wrong one, and is likely to cause more harm than good. He said seek out professional counselors and work with them to put your life back in order." The woman, barely audible, sniffed out a quiet thank you. The man said "What do you know?" and slammed the door as they walked away struggling with the two cases of beer. The look on his face and his prancing around with his loud mouth, prattling on about the incident, pretending he was seeking justice for his female friend, which was in reality, just a way to capitalized on this heart wrenching opportunity for sexual gratification. I just hoped she heeded my words to protect herself from this sexual predator.

Barriers

*E*very once in a while some dimwitted, overpaid, bureaucrat comes to realize that their contribution to the taxi industry they represent, is nil. So, in order to justify their existence, he or she attempts to come up with a policy that will dazzle their bosses and protect them from rightful dismissal. They go to great lengths to sell their idea to their employer, which may seem ingenious at the time, but, eventually, spells disaster and, in some cases, may be fatal to those concerned. Such was the case when some brainless bureaucrat came up with the idea of pushing the cab industry to install bullet-proof glass protectors, separating passengers from their drivers. The idea was to provide safety and protection from robbery, assault, or other forms of abuse for drivers. It didn't do any of those things at all. In fact, it had the opposite effect and nobody could figure out why. I remember the buzz in the office and in the news in general, that had everybody talking. Cabbies who installed these new barriers were conned into feeling a false sense of security. Some echoed statements that translated their message to the taxi riders which said," I dare you to try any of your crap on me now, buddy!"

I remember watching our company manager on the six o'clock news driving around with a reporter during their interview. Right from the start I knew that this idea would never fly. Barriers might be a good idea in large American cities like New York, Chicago, or L.A. where people shoot you while chomping on a drippy hot dog. However, we in Canada do not live with a bang bang shoot-em up cowboy mentality. We don't sleep with a gun under our pillows and we wouldn't use one to eliminate someone even if we did. Besides being an expensive proposition, barriers only encouraged confrontations between the drivers and their passengers. In the first week of installation, there was a reported sharp increase in violent attacks on the cabbies and incidences of fares not paying their driver. So right from the beginning, problems arose that proved detrimental to the taxi industry in general. I remember telling a taxicab board employee that, "When you place a barrier between the cab driver and the passenger, everything changes. You eliminate that personal element and replace it with one of threat and challenge. The short time a passenger spends with their driver is a personal, intimate, one. Usually, it's the time when the two parties engage in lighthearted conversation, maybe share a joke or two, and sometimes, it's an opportunity for the passenger to unload their problems. This is kind of like the interaction that occurs in a bar between the bartender and the patron they're serving. In a taxi however, the interchange is carried at a more secure and higher personal level. The interaction sails along in a secure non-threatening environment. Usually, the conversation is pleasant and stimulating. The length of time the two parties spend interacting in a cab is generally short, yet, satisfying. When you change that scenario by placing a barrier in the vehicle with that non-spoken sense of intimidation: trouble is the result. I remember one of the company's mild mannered veteran drivers being assaulted, then robbed the very first week he had it installed! I was shocked. It affirmed what I believed to be true. Barriers do just that. They place a barrier between you and your customer. For the ones who feel threatened or challenged at any level, look out! Now your job is not pleasant anymore, now that personal touch is gone! These barriers, bullet-proof or not, are a harbinger of trouble and menace. After a period of time the shields were removed from all the taxis in the city of Winnipeg and sanity prevailed.

I drove taxi for twenty odd years in Winnipeg and I never had a violent or abusive encounter with any of my passengers. I love people and I love exchanging ideas with them and find myself often fascinated listening to their experiences. I believe people just want to be treated with respect and a little compassion. After all, isn't that what we all want?

Mournful Rider

eople experience and express grief differently. One early clear, sunny summer morning I drove a middle aged lady to a cemetery somewhere near Bird's Hill Park. It was a peaceful ride and I was enjoying our conversation. She seemed happy as we talked and chatted all the way to the cemetery. She told me that she was going to visit her husband's grave and pay her respects. She seemed in control of her emotions and even laughed once in a while. I had never been to Bird's Hill Park cemetery before, so I rather enjoyed the drive. Once I arrived at the cemetery she directed me to the site of her husband's grave. It was near the edge of the narrow asphalt road. I pulled over and shut off the car. She walked to the headstone but it wasn't until she reached it that she fell to her knees and broke down and wailed in pain; crying uncontrollably. I was taken aback at how, as if on cue, she lost control and unleashed her emotions. I watched as she spoke and I tried my best not to eavesdrop because for this woman, in her early sixties, it was personal. Fifteen minutes later she returned to the car and I drove away. The drive back was a little more solemn and calm.

Lonely Widow Expresses Grief

One evening in the middle of the week, I drove an older lady home to an address on Magnus Avenue in the north end. When she paid me she accidently gave me an extra five dollar bill. When I realized what she had done and pointed it out to her, she looked at me with pain in her eyes and told me that she had recently lost her husband, so she had a lot of things on her mind. It was obvious she was still in mourning. With a pathetically sad look on her face, one resigned to pain, said, "What's this world all about anyway?" She thanked me profusely and it seemed to mean so much to her and I was happy I had chosen to be honest. It would have been so easy to simply pocket the bill into my shirt and say good-by. She probably wouldn't have even noticed but I know God noticed, because I still get a good feeling about it whenever I think about it even after all these years.

Visit to a Chronic Care Facility

I was a young man when I first started driving a taxi in Winnipeg and I have to admit that I thought it absurd to think that a man would physically break down and cry, for any reason. I thought I was too macho to ever shed a tear for any reason, other than when a close friend or family member dies. It seems it's an unwritten law among young men that says, 'big boys don't cry'. That changed the day that the dispatcher sent me way down St. Mary's Road to pick up a nurse and drive her back to her home in East Kildonan. I walked through those big glass doors and made my way up to the second floor. I remember that it was unlike a regular hospital in that it was quiet, like a library. There were no doctors and nurses running around in a state of panic, trying to resolve medical emergencies. There were no alarms blaring away or voices coming over the public address system, calling personnel to certain stations, or for someone to call a

212

certain number. I was told by my dispatcher that this was a special hospital. That was a gross understatement. I saw a patient parked in his wheelchair against a wall quiet as a mouse. At first, I thought he was dead but on closer inspection I noticed that this almost lifeless patient was a neatly dressed man and, if you looked closely, you could see his chest moving as he took shallow breaths. He sat still like a mannequin with no expression on his face. Like a zombie! The biggest shocker came when I noticed he had no bottom jaw. I saw other residents in similar or worse conditions. As I walked past patients rooms, I saw patients who, for all intents and purposes, were vegetables. The healthiest patient I saw was gurgling something incoherently as he stared out at nothing. Like most of the other patients, he was unable to stand, move, or walk. Some drooled incessantly soaking their shirts or attached bibs. I couldn't even imagine what it would be like to have to feed them or even, watch them eat. The passenger, who I was supposed to pick up, found me in the hall searching for the way to get out. I was visibly shaken. She waved me over to her, and together we scurried out the front doors and marched to my waiting taxi. I hustled myself behind the wheel and put the car in drive but as soon as I touched the gas my fare held up her index finger in the air, indicating for me to stop, which I did immediately. She had forgotten something from her office. I was glad that she did, because I needed a few alone minutes to compose myself. I took the time to pray, something I hadn't done in years! It gave me the time I needed to release a flood of tears. I thanked God for blessing me with a healthy body. I prayed that I would never forget that wonderful gift. I remembered the words of a prophet I had read in the Bible who said. "But for the grace of God, walk I. All I could say to that was, Amen! When the passenger returned she could see I was upset and she gently placed her hand on my shoulder and looked me in the eye with the most understanding look anyone had ever given me. Neither of us spoke for the longest time. We cried silently together. Neither of us spoke a word but somehow we didn't need to. We somehow understood the moment. I was nearly home and both of us composed when she said, "All people have a right to live even when that person lives life in a diminished capacity! In some societies these people were abandoned in the wilderness among wild beasts, killed, or simply annihilated. The lucky ones lived in pathetic institutions where they were beaten, sexually abused, or used as guinea pigs for strange experiments. The best that we've got for them now is to make their lives comfortable and to provide them with all necessary forms of protection. It's hell, I know, but I tell myself that when they leave this world, heaven awaits." Maybe I'm delusional in my thinking, but I choose to believe that, you should too. It works for me she said with finality in her voice. She leaned across and hugged me then hopped out of my taxi. Nothing more needed to be said.

Main Street Disasters

*A*s I shared earlier, I grew up in the frosty northern Ontario town of Kirkland Lake. I had many friends growing up there and some of them were close friends who happened to be native. I was in for a culture shock when I moved to Winnipeg. Soon, I observed the violent lifestyle of the natives whenever I cruised up or down Main Street. It was the talk of the town! That observation was greatly accelerated when I started driving taxi. Once I drove taxi, that mayhem became up close and personal. In those days, life on the street was mayhem and murder, and the role of the cops was to clean up the blood, puke, urine, and scrape bodies off the streets before the press took pictures of the carnage or worse, written about it in their newspapers. It was a macabre reality. My friends and I use to make jokes about it. None of us had ever seen such a sight on any street before. There were bars on both side of the street and every one of them, was doing a booming business. The

215

white man, I assume was capitalizing on the aboriginal's addictions. It was exploitation perfected to a science. I never knew who owned those establishments way back then, and I still don't, but I picture some lawyer, doctor, or businessman with lots of money at their disposal, being a secret or silent owner. I've always wondered about that and I'm sure it would be a shocking surprise to a lot of people if they knew who those owners were or are now. I read those bright neon signs flashing in their windows that said, "DANCING NIGHTLY" We put in our own interpretation of those signs. We laughingly injected the words, "FIGHTING HOURLY!" and, in reality, it was that violent on the streets. It wasn't unusual to see a brawl or fist fight going on along Main Street every hundred feet. Males or females! It was all the same. One night, outside a Main Street bar, I watched two native women in their thirties, fist fighting while a group of a dozen men or so, looking on and cheering. They had big smiles on their faces, proof that they were thoroughly enjoying the entertainment. Nobody attempted to stop the brutal altercation. As in all brutal fights of this nature, one dominates while the other, falls victim to their assailant. I observed one woman fall and bump her head on the cement sidewalk, landing unconscious. She ended up immobile, flat on her back, on the edge of the sidewalk with her head dangling aimlessly over the curb, like a ball on a cord, the kind boxers practice on as they pummel the leather head shaped bag making it sound like an electric drum. The victor wasted no time in sealing her victory by administering a flurry of brutal kicks to the head of the victim as she laid there helplessly. I was surprised by the agility that the native woman was able to deliver those kicks. This wasn't her first fight! That seemed to have gotten the biggest reaction from the crowd. Some of them cheered as they marched with arms around the victor's shoulder, like they would a boxer who had knocked out their opponent. All headed into the nearby bar for a victory drink. It was disgusting and I quickly drove away, disgusted with myself for watching and feeling cowardly for doing nothing. I radioed the dispatcher to send the police to the scene. The woman died in the hospital the next day from a concussion. I remember thinking, what a stupid and uncivilized way to live. What a waste I said, when I heard it over the news channel the next day.

Over the years I have seen many people stabbed on Main Street, none of them wanted a ride to the hospital. They stoically hopped out of my cab, oblivious to their open knife wounds, with their flesh gaping open. They simply silently disappeared into the night to who knows where. I suppose to some of them it was a source of fascinating war stories they would later share with anyone who would listen. There were many rumors and stories abounding in and around Main Street but all the ones in this book I witnessed or heard first hand from the horse's mouth, so to speak.

Knuckle Sandwich

*P*rior to working at Red Taxi, I was employed at a battery factory in St. James. I worked from 4 pm until 12:30 a.m. After my shift I walked down to the corner of Ellis and Ferry Road to catch my bus back to East Kildonan. Most nights the bartender who worked at the Airport Hotel, located right at that bus stop, caught that same bus to Portage and Donald. One night I overheard the following narrative from that bartender who loudly proclaimed it to the bus driver and everyone else within earshot on the bus, as we headed home. He was saying that he once worked as a bartender at the Occidental Hotel on Main Street. He said that the place was always super busy and volatile. This one particular evening he told about two native men who got into a full blown fist fight near the crowded dance floor. He said that they were rolling around like two fools punching, kicking, scratching, and grabbing anything they could throw at each other. He said that somehow, one combatant managed to clamp down onto

218

the hand of the other fighter and sucked his index finger into his mouth and started to bite down hard on it. He severed the finger of the dominant fool just below the knuckle of his left hand. A couple of bouncer's appeared and threw the two brawlers out into the street. Then they brought out the mops and pails and cleaned up the mess. In no time the drinking and dancing continued as if nothing had happened. One of the bartenders was so disgusted by what he saw, that he immediately took off his apron, retrieved his coat from behind the bar and stormed out. This place is a zoo, he said in disgust! How can people live like this!

Occidental Hotel

When I decided to move to Winnipeg, two of my closest friends followed along with me and both of them were accomplished musicians. They had formed a band back home and played at regular high school gigs and various dance halls in Northern Ontario. A year after settling in Winnipeg they met other musicians who were looking for new members to form a band. They were gladly accepted and played at various bars throughout the city. After a few months, their agent, taking advantage of their naivety, booked them a gig at the Occidental Hotel for one full week. When Robert, the lead guitarist, told me the news, I roared with laughter in his face. Although I was relatively new to driving taxi in the city, I was well aware of the life that went on at various bars in Winnipeg and I knew that the Occidental had the worst reputation in terms of violence and absurd anti social behaviour flaunted about shamelessly. Incidences, like stabbings, murders, male and female fistfights, open sexual activity in its many forms. It was a zoo and when they told me they were going to be working there for a whole week, the first thing I asked Robert was if I could have his Fender guitar when he gets stabbed to death. I was only slightly exaggerating; the truth is that the reality of it was literal. At the end of the week when we three friends were at home Robert, and Ray, the other musician, we talked about their experience, having played six nights at the Occidental Hotel. He spoke with real disgust and scoffed when describing the scene. "It was brutal!" said Robert as he shared the scene with me. "One night I saw this young native man with long hair passed out at the table with his head resting on his folded arms. A bouncer bigger than Hulk Hogan walked up to the table and grabbed the chair where the unconscious man sat. He grabbed the back of the chair and spun it around with so much force that the young man remained in the exact position except that now he faced the heavy wooden exit door. The native had no idea what was going on. The greasy bouncer then slammed his huge hands down hard on the back of the aboriginal's head and immediately ran with gusto toward the exit. Though unconscious, the native had no choice but to run along behind him. When he reached those doors, the bouncer used the native's head as a battering ram, busting outside and sent him splayed on the sidewalk where he didn't move a muscle. I thought he was dead!" Robert told me. It surprised him because the reaction of the crowd was one of passive indifference. No one reacted. No one said a word. No one protested nor did anyone attempt to help the native and those that were dancing kept dancing, not missing a step. "This happened many times during the course of the evening!" my disgusted friend said. He told me there was blood on the dance floor and that it wasn't surprising to see patrons with blood covered faces and bloody clothes. The only constant was the music that blared in the place, a death knell of sorts. The place buzzed none stop and the riff raff kept coming. The Occidental Hotel attracted their violent clientele like a hive attracts killer bees. These things described above were typical in the patrons it attracted.

Another Front Page Headline: It wasn't just aboriginals that got caught up in the daily grind of the Occidental. In my own observation I found that the rowdiest patrons who frequented in and around the Occidental were the so called white men who worked way up north in no man's land and earning generous isolation pay. They usually came to town after spending six months in pent up energy. Then they would come to town with thousands of dollars stuffed in their pockets ready to let loose. And boy did they let loose! These men were the orneriest, loudest, most violent and most womanizing of them all. I actually met one of them who arrived in town on a Friday night, with forty five hundred dollars in his pockets. That same man was flat broke by Sunday evening. They had to call their boss at their base camp and arrange transportation to get back home so they could get back to work for Monday morning. You really have to use your imagination to figure out how they did that; some of it certainly was illegal I'm sure! One Friday evening, around nine o'clock, two plain clothes cops sat in an unmarked cop car at the curb in front of the Occidental Hotel. It was a nice June evening as the cops sat with their windows down enjoying the warm night air. There was a lot of traffic on the street thus making the sidewalks busy giving it a carnival like atmosphere. Four men walking along as a group, walked casually by the cops sitting at the curb outside the main entrance to the occidental Hotel. As the group sauntered past the cop car the officer called on of the man, *faggot.* Naturally the group quickly gathered at the passenger window where a heated argument broke out between the walkers and the cops. Some punches were thrown and one of the men from the group made the mistake of pulling out a knife and stabbed the officer in the chest. The officer then pulled out his gun and started firing into the group. Two men of the group died on the sidewalk and one was left in critical condition. Soon a dozen cop cars showed up on the scene then a couple ambulances. It was pandemonium to say the least.

Bloody Sunday

I share these stories with you, the reader, as a precursor to an incident I happened upon one warm, sunny Sunday. Of course it happened on Main Street. But it didn't happen on a day or night when I was driving my cab. However I think it solidifies and puts into perspective the dark life that exists on the streets and in the lives of aboriginals, who step into a new, unfriendly, exploitive society from a world from which they exited. This story is graphic, tragic, sad, but most horrifyingly true. All of these elements have been burnt onto the souls of these native people mercilessly, from day one. Read on.

After a hectic week of driving cab including putting in a twenty hour shift on Friday, I stayed awake after my Friday shift and took a nice long bath, shaved, then, I had an early supper. I climbed into bed and fell soundly asleep early Saturday evening. I was in la la land before my head hit the pillow. I slept twelve beautiful hours and when I awoke Sunday morning, I felt invigorated. The sun brightly lit up my room as if I were posing for a photo shoot for some glamour magazine. I didn't work Sundays so, I felt great knowing I had the whole day for myself and my wife to enjoy together. I snuggled up to my wife and enjoyed the time with the thought that I wanted us to do something enjoyable. After a while we got up and had an early breakfast. We caught up on the latest news and played some of our popular records, enjoying the memories that they evoked.

It was one of those lazy days of summer. It wasn't quite warm enough to go to the beach so we decided to take in a matinee downtown. We wanted to relax and enjoy ourselves in an air conditioned theatre. We drove downtown to the cinema off Portage and Donald. Now, I forget what movie we had seen that day but I do remember that it was a good one, and we thoroughly enjoyed it.

After the movie we made our way to our car and drove up Princess to Higgins Avenue. When we drove within sight of the intersection at Logan and Main Street, I saw a swarm of cops and police cruisers with their red lights flashing. I caught a flash of Kresge's brick building with an inordinate amount of blood splattered on its brick wall, on the Logan side of the street. The only thing that I could guess might have happened to cause so much carnage was that a motorist must have raced through the intersection at Main and Logan, lost control of his vehicle, then drove into a pedestrian or two who just happened to be walking there at the time. There was blood everywhere. Because I wanted to see the whole picture for myself I intentionally turned right on Logan and headed toward the Disraeli freeway. There was a policeman directing traffic at Main Street because the accident and the blood had attracted so many inquisitive onlookers. Drivers passing by the horrific scene were stretching their necks to maximum capacity for a better look, slowing down traffic to a crawl from all directions. I'm ashamed now to say I had joined that throng of rubber neckers, adding chaos to the scene. Because I was forced to crawl along so slowly, I got a front row seat to the entire crime scene. I have never seen so much blood in one place at one time in all my entire life. The only place that would have yielded more blood would have been if I would have entered the killing floor at Maple Leaf Foods. The sidewalk was covered with blood and the only time I ever saw that much liquid on the street, was after a vicious thunderstorm when the water level on the street reaches the curb. So it was now, with that huge volume of liquid. My wife could not look at the sight at all and covered her eyes. Even I gagged and had to look away. The last image I caught as I floored it past the lights was a cop with a rag covering his mouth. It was a ghastly scene and it wasn't until the next day when I was talking with a police friend of mine in a coffee shop, that he gave me the whole story as to what happened.

Apparently, it being such a warm beautiful day these three native friends were staggering around looking for a way to get hold of some alcohol. Finally, they collaborated and dug deep into their pockets for every penny they could find. Between the three of them, they came up with just enough cash to purchase a bottle of Lysol. Unfortunately, friend number one decided to run home nearby to see if he could find some more money to buy more alcohol. Friend number one returned a little later and met up with his two compatriots only to find out that they had already consumed the Lysol. They didn't wait for their friend to join them to complete the party. This sent the excluded friend into a murderous rage. Tragically, for the duo, there was a short piece of two by four lying flat on the sidewalk against the Kresge's building. He immediately picked up the length of wood and attacked his two friends with it so severely that they needed dental records to eventually identify the bodies. For the longest time I had a difficulty sleeping. I had to learn to put it out of my mind in order to allow myself to relax enough to fall asleep. I believe this illustrates or underlines the results that can happen when you take a nation of people, pay them a pittance to keep themselves hidden in the wilderness. We then take away their dignity, kidnap their children, send them off to residential boarding schools into the waiting arms of pedophiles and other predatory sickos. Then, for the sake of money and greed, introduce them to a world of alcohol and drugs and the white man's rules, when they show up on our streets. When they inevitably get into trouble with the law, we quickly throw them in jail. It's no secret. Shame on us!!

Overreaction to Rip Off Pair

*I*t doesn't matter how savvy you may be as a taxi driver or how precautious you may become. No matter how many years of driving you have under your belt, sooner or later a fare will rip you off. Accept it, it happens to every driver, some more than others. No one appreciates getting ripped off by their fare and I didn't like it much either. So I came up with my own vigilante method for handling such situations.

Like my very first experience of getting ripped off by the smooth criminal who spotted how naïve I was and simply stated that he had already paid me, even though he hadn't. From that experience I decided I wouldn't let that happen to me ever again. I took off my rose colored glasses for good. I quickly learned that if I wanted to be a cab driver, I would have to get dirty once in a while. Whenever a fare refused to pay me I went into my prepared monologue that went something like this. Now

I have to say that I am not a violent man but I felt that if I wanted to survive as a cab driver I would have to have some sort of strategy. I would quickly and aggressively pull my cab over to the side of the road and say, in as threatening a voice possible say, "If I wanted to get into a career of fighting for my money by rolling around in the dirt, getting my clothes dirty and torn, I'd have chosen a career in the WWF where I would earn a lot more money. So, if I am going have to fight you in order to get paid, I'm going to make it worth my while,!" unlike my first experience of waiting for hours for the cops to show up, I go into my aggression act. I don't call cops. I do something much better. First, I will pull you out of my car and we will fight tooth and nail. Sometimes I will lose the fight but most often, I will win; but like I said, either way, I will make it worth my while. If I win I'm going to work you over real good. I'll knock most of your teeth out of your mouth and break your jaw in a few places. I'm going to make sure you spend at least a few days in the hospital. When the doctors patch you up you'll look like a mummy. Then, whatever amount of money you have on you, I'm taking every penny of it! Most often when people refused to pay me it almost always turned out that they had more than enough cash to cover their fare, sometime over a hundred dollars. I'm also going to take your ring, your wrist watch, your coat, your shoes or boots as well as any other items of value you may have in your possession!" Most of the time the tough talk is all I needed and the customer often mysteriously found the money to pay for the fare. The odd time I have had to quickly scramble out of my cab with the keys in my pocket and follow through on my threats. Over time I amassed a collection of watches, rings and occasionally, items of clothing. I didn't have to fight very often and not for long. I was in pretty good shape way back then, but, I do have to admit, I occasionally took a beating.

One near fighting episode happened one snowy night on Portage Avenue across from the University of Winnipeg. I picked up two men in their early twenties and drove them to St. Mary's Road. When I got there, they said they had no money. I suspected that they thought that they were going to clean up on me, since the odds were two to one. I lost it. I pulled over to the curb, quickly slammed on my brakes, and slammed my right palm on the man's chest, who was sitting next to me in the front seat. I held him pinned to the seat with enough force that he couldn't move and the other man in the back froze where he was! I went through my threatening spiel with enough conviction in my voice that when I told them to hand over their coats, they did. Because I was so angry at the time, I ordered the guy in the front seat to hand over his new steel toed boots he was wearing as well. Then I kicked them out of my cab even though it was getting to the end of winter on a cold snowy night. I drove off leaving them in a hail of slush and ice on the sidewalk, without a thing on their backs or footwear. As

I drove past Eaton's I remembered that the coat from my front seat passenger looked brand new, which I guessed was stolen. It was a beautiful pig skin jacket which sold for $387 at Eaton's. I drooled over it when I'd first seen it on the rack. I knew I couldn't even dream of buying it for myself. Remember, this was 1970 and the minimum wage was $1.25 an hour. The other item of clothing I secured from the second passenger was a corduroy jacket worth about $75, probably stolen as well. The hard toed boots were probably worth $75. Altogether I had scored about $500 for a four dollar fare. By this time I had cooled down enough for my conscience to kick in. I felt sick to my stomach because I realized I was wrong to do what I did. It was overkill at best. I turned around and headed back up Portage Avenue with the intention of returning all those items back to those two men. I searched desperately up St. Mary's Road to find them but my efforts were in vain. This incident made me feel bad because I knew it was not the right thing to do. I kept that in mind at other times when my fare had no money to pay me. A friend, to whom I confided this incident, told me that it was okay to be angry at times like these but, I should try *controlled* anger! Sometimes, it's okay to drive away ripped off, it's psychologically healthy and you'll sleep better because your conscience is clear. From that point on I did just that.

Poison Darts!

*P*oison darts! 'WHAAAT?' What are they? I am relating to incidences that I have seen occur in my taxi many times over the years. I'm talking about the most crippling form of child abuse, actually any form of abuse any human can inflict on one human being to another. The kind that stings the deepest and stays on our souls forever! I'm talking about verbal abuse and I think this story well illustrates my meaning. Words sting like poison darts where they penetrate the soul and fester there forever. But they don't just fester, they radiate our psyche with growing intensity, like radiation poison, until the person or victim concerned is affected until they gasp out their last breath before they leave this world. Read on! Be aware! One instance in particular happened around the fifteenth of December. I was happy at heart that the weather reflected the time of year that it was. It was comfortably cold but my mood was uplifted when I watched in awe, the huge butterfly snowflakes descending sleepily to the earth

233

from moisture filled clouds. A short time before noon, I was dispatched to pick up a fare. It was a mother and her two young boys from a low rental district on the east side of town and I drove them to another low rental place, on Keenleyside Drive. They were dressed in frayed thread bare clothing, obviously items picked up from recycling bins or items that had been handed down to them from strangers to those who were in great need. In spite of the near freezing weather, neither boy wore mitts, ear muffs, toques, boots or even socks. I could see their filthy little feet through their worn out summer running shoes. I shivered for the boys when a gust of wind blew over everyone as they slowly made their way to the car. The boys wore thin spring jackets that did nothing to protect them from the blustery wind. The trio emerged from the front door of their home as soon as I pulled up in front. Each boy carried an overstuffed shopping bag with their mother unleashing a litany of abusive curse words aimed at the young boys. I couldn't make out the mothers words at first, until I had made a complete stop and got out to lend assistance. I guessed the mother to be in her mid to late twenties. I learned that the boys were six and nine, respectively. She also carried a couple of grocery store bags stuffed with dirty broken toys. She was furious about something, though I didn't know what. She roared loudly cursing out her two boys mercilessly. Her graphic curse words and other barbed idioms cut through the air like poison darts, landing devastatingly on their young sensitive hearts. The words reverberated through the air like jet fighters unleashing their destroying payload on the boys who were just there with no protective armor to shield them from the devastation. Each word cut like a knife, penetrating the tender spirits of the boys, mercilessly. Things flew from her arms as she vehemently roared her displeasure, directing her rage, first at the boys, then at the boy's father, who, sadly, wasn't there at the time.

"Stop playing around you little bastards!" her words exploding out of her mouth. I don't need your rotten attitudes to add to your alcoholic lazy ass father. He ruined my life! I wanted to send you to live with your good for nothing drunken father but he doesn't want you either! You're too freaking bad! He hates your guts and wants nothing to do with you! He won't spend a penny on you for your support because you're not important to him! He doesn't give a rat's ass about either one of you!" He hates you and couldn't care less about you!" She repeated this phrase over and over again, stressing her words with as much emphasis she could muster. The boys remained silent but I could see the looks of devastation on their faces as they fumbled with their bags, as they climbed into the back seat. The boys kept their heads down with eyes focused on the snow covered earth. There's no Christmas for you guys this year!" she screamed with finality. 'You're lazy, useless, father wants to drink beer and stay drunk for Christmas. He said screw you when I asked him about your Christmas presents! He doesn't love you! He doesn't give a crap about you, period! So forget about Santa bringing you anything because your father doesn't care!" I was floored by this awful mother's rantings. As the youngest boy passed by me to hop in the back. I noticed a tear escape his eyes and silently streak down his cheek. The six year old boy got into the back seat while the nine year old got into the back from the passenger side. Both boys moved about mechanically, their moods dark and somber. I made my way to the passenger side and opened the door for the mother, though my heart wasn't in it. It surprised me when she said thank you, then got in and slammed her door shut. The first civilized word she spoke since she emerged from her house. She told me her destination and I started to move along but her ranting started over again with the same abusive and graphic intensity that she had expressed earlier. I couldn't stand to see her destroy her sons any longer so I pulled over to the curb and came to an abrupt stop. "That's more abuse than I want to hear in one day! Can't you see the pain and hurt you're heaping on your kids!?" I stormed at her. She started to retaliate at my word but I cut her off immediately. "Shut up!" I roared. It was my turn to rant. "I'm sorry about your husband but, whatever his problem is; it's not the boy's fault! I shouted. I didn't want to get into a lengthy discussion so I moved into the ultimatum part of my little rant. "If you don't stop this abuse right now, I will contact he children's Aid as soon as you leave this cab and, believe me, there will be consequences to pay! On that note I stopped talking and waited for her to respond but everything was quiet in the taxi. After a few seconds I resumed driving and continued to her destination, my heart beating a mile a minute. I was greatly relieved when they exited my cab, though my heart still ached for those two young victims, three counting the mother. It affected me so much, that 30 years later, it is as clear as the day it happened, and I still get an ache in my heart when I think about it.

Cheater's Remorse

I don't know what it is about some men, that when they are unsure about their sweetheart's love and devotion, even under the promise of marriage, sometimes, tend to facilitate or orchestrate proof of that love by allowing a test of that love, as dysfunctional as that may sounds. That's what I seemed to have walked into one late Friday night.

Actually, it was really Saturday, 3:30 a.m. I picked up a good looking young woman who I guessed was in her late twenties. When I arrived at the front door of the three story apartment building on Talbot Avenue, the woman was sobbing uncontrollably as her male friend helped her into the taxi. She looked as if she had just woken up from a drunken sleep as she was terribly disheveled. It was obvious to me that, whatever was going on, alcohol definitely played a part in it. The woman tried to walk on her own but couldn't. She was unsteady on her feet, and had a hard time to focus. Mr. Macho man kept a contented smile on his face the whole time, and had to help her all the way into the back seat of the cab. Her hair was sticking out in all directions. It looked like she had slept in her clothes. Because her speech was slurred it was difficult to understand to what degree or level of drunkenness she was at, as her sobs overrode her words. Her shirtless macho male companion held a crooked snide grin, and reminded me of the proverbial cat who swallowed the canary. He tossed the woman's purse into the back seat of the taxi, and then closed the door.

As I drove the pretty young woman home, her sobbing continued and I was concerned that maybe she had been sexually assaulted, so I asked her if she wanted me to drive her to the police station or a hospital but she declined the offer. A little later when she had calmed down a bit I asked her what happened, thinking that maybe her date had gone bad, but it wasn't that at all. Her story clarified things. She told me that she had met a man some months ago, whom she fell madly in love with, and soon became engaged to be married sometime that summer. It turned out that they both knew her old boyfriend. I don't know how it came about but somehow, her old boyfriend convinced her fiancé that his sweetheart was really in love with *him* and if given half a chance he could prove it by spending an intimate evening with her in his bed. Her fiancé said "Oh yeah try it and you'll see, you haven't got a hope". Apparently, that's exactly what happened. The old boyfriend took the dare and she ended up waking up in her old sweetheart's

239

bed at that awful hour of that morning. She was drunk, but not so drunk that she couldn't remember all the events of the evening. She said she had fallen asleep and her ex boyfriend woke her up and told her to get herself together and get out. He did not want her there. So he helped her gather her things and called a taxi. That whole thing was just to prove a point on his side.

I had a few questions of my own to ask her but I didn't want to add to her misery. I figured she had enough anguish to deal with in terms of a potentially angry fiancé who would show up the next day. All I could think to say is that whatever happened that evening was a silly game that neither she, nor her fiancé, should have even entertained. Also, alcohol can, and does, make fools of us all at times, so try to deal positively with it. Everybody makes mistakes. I wondered how her fiancé would fare under the same set of circumstances. What if she had set up her good looking girlfriend to seduce her man? Would he come out unscathed? Let's not find out I told her! I didn't know how she was going to handle her dilemma but I felt sorry for her.

Fighting Warriors

I've seen a lot of fights along Main Street over the years, some of them quite brutal and bloody. I've seen middle aged men walking home in the Selkirk area overpowered by some young punks who would knock them down then grab their beer and run off with it. Sometimes the perpetrator was a lone male and sometimes it was two or more punks, bent on committing the same crime, beer being the motivating factor. On one occasion 1 witnessed what 1 perceived to be, two evenly matched combatants. In this case, beer was not a motivating factor, rather, survival of the fittest was. This happened on north Main Street, on the east side just two blocks north of Jarvis Street. These two young adult men had each other by the throat, one pinning the other against a dirty brick wall. Neither man had any backup or an accomplice to help them out. They were each left to their own strengths. It was almost boring to watch. One of the pugilists would punch his assailant with a flurry of punches to the head until he got tired. Then he would stop and rest a minute to catch his breath. At this point his opponent would release a wild flurry of punches of his own until he got tired and had to rest. This exchange of punches relayed back and forth for a long time with neither fighter defeated, nor defeating the other. In each exchange of punches, about a dozen of them landed. In each case I thought whoever was on the receiving end would fall, but not so. After a brief rest, the other fighter would, in turn land a few haymakers of his own and I thought he would be victorious, but not so. Eventually, I lost interest and drove away. Let these two fools beat themselves into oblivion I thought to myself, after all they're just stupid enough to become friends!

The Christmas Present

The world looked like a snow globe that late Friday night after the bars had closed, three weeks before Christmas. Afar off I noticed a lone gentleman standing outside the McLaren Hotel carrying a large, fancy wrapped Christmas gift under his arm. He wore a light colored trench coat, a fedora, and leather gloves. He wore what looked like freshly dry cleaned dress pants, with new winter ski boots on his feet. There was no indication that he was intoxicated as he seemed pretty steady on his feet. My first thought was that he was one of the staff from the hotel looking for a ride home after his shift. I knew the buses had stopped running hours ago and hailing down a cab was the only option left to him. Where he waited, at that particular corner, was not the ideal area for him to hang around especially with a fancy wrapped Christmas gift tucked under his arm. He was more likely to attract unwanted attention. He was obviously and anxiously on the look-out for a taxi. He kept searching nervously in every direction for something. When I approached the curb where he stood he beamed with relief. He wasted no time opening my door and instantly asked if I could take him home. I inquired as to where he was going and he quickly answered with an address way down Pembina Highway. A twenty dollar fare for sure (which was almost unheard of in those days). It's my lucky day, I thought! He settled into the front seat with the gift positioned securely on his lap. I looked at the box and I concluded that whoever wrapped that gift put a lot of time and effort into the task. It was fancy, expensive looking wrapping paper intertwined with what looked like aluminum foil. A fancy silver ribbon circled the box tied on the top with a huge red bow. The present occupied the greater part of our conversation while on route.

He spoke with glowing excitement as he told me that this Christmas, was going to be an extraordinary one for it had been years since he had spent Christmas with his daughter. He spoke enthusiastically about the contents inside, what looked like, an oversized shoe box. He told his daughter that this year, she could get whatever she asked for. It just so happened that her dream gift was a Sony stereo. He told me how he added a white silk blouse with Peter Pan collars as well as a hundred dollars of Avon products. "It broke me" he said "but this year was special." He quieted down a moment as if digesting the glow of it all. Was he regretting his lavish spending on gifts for his daughter and was he now worried how far it set him back. After a few moments he perked up and said to me, "I once drove a cab myself a few years ago in Calgary and I know how people try to rip you off with bull crap stories like, "wait right here while I go inside my house to get the money to pay you. Then they never come back."

"Ya."I said, "It's the oldest trick in the book and I've been rooked more times than I care to remember." He seemed to consider this and answered, "Me too buddy, many, many times." He continued after a moment. "When we get there, I have to run in and get the money for the fare. To prove to you that I'm not going to run out on the fare I will leave this expensive gift on your seat while I run inside." Then he spoke solemnly saying, "If you take off with this present, I'll hunt you down and press charges, but I'll lay a severe beating on you first," he threatened. He then pulled out a coiled pocket note pad and wrote down my name, license number, address, phone number and all other information he could gather. Before he walked away from the taxi to walk toward his door, he stopped long enough to write down the number of the taxi, repeating loud enough so that half the condo dwellers could hear it. His last words were of warning, "Don't take off now! I'll only be a minute or two.

Based on our lengthy discussion on his daughter's gift I guessed it had to be worth four or five hundred dollars! The more I thought about it, the more I hoped he wouldn't come back. I mentally imagined who I could distribute the spoils of war to, if that became the case.

I waited 10 minutes but he didn't return. I waited half an hour more but there was still no sign of him. I realized that he wasn't coming back. Instead of feeling angry, I was glad because it meant that the Christmas present was now mine! I left as quickly and quietly as I could, without drawing attention to myself.

By the time I returned to Elmwood, I was excited and joyfully anxious to open that expensive gift. I pulled into the vacant parking lot at the Safeway grocery store. My mind raced with anticipation trying to determine who I would divide the spoils of war with, once I opened the present. I can give all those Avon items to my wife! I will send that blouse to my sister because she loves blouses with Peter Pan collars. As for the expensive stereo, I'll keep that one for myself! I was adamant in my mental allotment of all that booty and I didn't feel a bit guilty about it. After all, I was the one whose hands these goods fell into! I settled myself under a lamp and aggressively tore into the package. I couldn't help thinking "What if it's empty?" but no, it was too heavy. My fingers trembled with excitement, but that immediately dissipated when I gasped at the contents of the fancy wrapped Christmas present. Inside the gift box were neatly stacked pieces of scrap wood two by fours. I couldn't believe it. I started to laugh out loud. It took a while for the con to sink in and how caught up I was in it. My greed had totally overtaken me. I sat for a long time while digesting the con this clever crook sprung on me. He had to be a master I thought to myself. I couldn't get mad at the guy for doing what he had done. I could only admire him for his creativity. I deserved what I got. If I could have, I would have shaken his hand and slapped him on the back in congratulations. I learned something about both of us that night and felt that affinity uniting us in some convoluted way. Best rip off ever, I thought to myself as I drove off. This was a classic!

Coca Cola Avenger

*W*hile on the subject of getting ripped off, there was a period of time when I went through a more passive aggressive stage of retribution. Not so much as a means of financial compensation, but as a means of vengeance. My first experience happened late one winter evening when I drove a car full of party goers to an apartment block near Arlington at Sergeant Avenue. The group got out of my cab and scurried into an old dilapidated six story building without paying me. I could see them spill into an apartment on the fifth floor, because they put on the light as they entered. In a state of anger, I went to the nearest 7-11 and bought a few bottles of coke. I then drove back and parked across the street from the building, all the while watching the group partying inside the apartment. I seized a bottle of coke and threw it up toward the 6th story window with all my strength. It smashed just left of the window of the old red painted brick wall. It exploded loudly though the partygoers were totally unaware of the attempted assault taking place. With renewed determination I aimed carefully at my target and threw the second bottle but this time, it landed to the right of the apartment window. Finally, with greater determination and focus of energy, I threw the third bottle of coke with the greatest strength I could muster at the party people in the apartment. This time the bottle landed smack dab dead centre of the window. The bottle exploded on impact, throwing fizz and glass everywhere in the apartment. I heard a woman scream when it happened. I immediately moved to my cab and rushed off before they could identify me. I knew I was out a few dollars but the feeling of vindication was worth it to me. I used this tactic a few more times over the next year leaving me with the same feeling of victory every time.

My final such act of reprisal happened one evening when a well dressed man simply told me he wasn't going to pay me. "Do you own this house?" I asked. "Yes I do." he answered. "Well, make sure that you keep your insurance premiums paid up to date because soon, I will be throwing a bottle of coke right through your pretty front picture window, which means you will have a hell of a mess to clean up in your living room! And who knows, maybe this might cause your premiums to go up." He didn't say a word but he studied me for a minute, at which time I continued. "I might do it tonight, tomorrow, next week, next month or even next year! Who knows when, just know that it will happen, I guarantee it!" In

249

conclusion I said, "Good bye Mr. Thief, get to hell out of my car, I'm busy." He slowly and silently crept out of my taxi, at which point, I spun out, showering him with gravel, mud, and water. Six weeks later, on a Friday night around three in the morning, I threw my final bottle of coke through that picture window. Like the bottle I first threw at the apartment on that frigid winter night, this one exploded as well but this time I threw a second bottle to underline to Mr. Thief, who had thrown the bottles. I then ran out from between two houses to my parked car, sitting two streets over. When I got into my taxi I calmly drove away. From then, on I resorted to other means to handle non paying fares. Fighting wasn't so bad.

Foiled Escape

I know not all my methods were fair but other cab drivers were downright brutal. I remember one late Friday night shortly after the bars had closed I dropped off a fare way up Henderson Highway. I walked through a low rental complex just in time to see a sickening spectacle. I recognized a young man whom I had seen flag down a Duffy's taxi a short time before. The driver had obviously tackled this young man and had him subdued and held him pinned on his knees so that he couldn't move. I got the gist of his predicament. He probably told the driver he had to run inside to get the money to pay him, but he tried to run. The driver had a firm grip on the beaten native man's long hair and had him poised like a golfer ready to tee off. The pathetic young man was beaten and he patiently waited for the final blow to be delivered. I appeared on the scene at the precise second the driver brutally and mercilessly kicked this young, helpless, man in the face, sending him reeling senseless onto his back. "F......g crook!," he said in disgust as he passed me, heading back to his cab and back to feeding grounds on Main Street. Thank goodness I could never resort to brutality like that, no matter how angry I got.

Solo Holliday

*E*arly one July morning I picked up an elderly classy lady at a pent house on Osborne and drove her to a ritzy high rise building on Valhalla Drive in North Kildonan. She told me that after paying a short visit to her husband's temporary residence, she and her best friend were going to meet, and from there, they would be continuing on to the airport. She told me that the two would then be off to Rome which, as is turned out, was going to be the first leg of their lengthy, luxurious European holiday. My first thoughts were, how callous and self centered a wife she was to just abandon her husband while she travelled the globe. However, I chose to shut up and just drive. I had learned a long time ago, it's always best to keep quiet and just listen. That way one can learn so much more and perhaps even save one from receiving a severe reprimand from time to time.

Soon after her friend Marla, showed up, the wealthy lady embraced her husband, and after a short visit, said good-by. Then the three of us made our way to the

253

waiting taxi parked outside, near the front lobby. There were no tears or arguments or spiteful words from either of them. I felt disturbed because of the cold send off I witnessed. It made me feel rather uncomfortable, but, it was none of my affair, period. The two friends engaged themselves in animated conversation all the way to the airport. I listened with interest but kept myself aloof from the discussion. I did manage to pick up a few items of interest I hadn't known before. She expressed her disappointment about her husband's decision to stay home. While initially, the wife was distraught and felt cheated, while her husband decided to temporarily rent a swanky apartment because, for the time being anyway, he looked forward to staying indoors. It was said of her husband that since his retirement, he enjoyed being alone on occasion. He planned to have some friends over for friendly games of poker, Canasta or rummoli! There were a lot of things he was looking forward to doing alone, now that he was going to have the chance! Heck, watch some TV, read a few books, take in a movie every once in a while! Maybe even reach out to some family members! There were a long list of things he had wanted to do and he refused to feel guilty about it. Her therapist told her to go alone or with a friend if that's what it had to be. "Enjoy yourself!" he told her. It wasn't the end of the world. It just might loosen things up at home, and heaven knows, there would be other opportunities for them to vacation together. Next year might be an entirely different scenario. "Don't worry about it till then!" he advised. Apparently, she followed his advice and convinced her friend to come along with her, on her dime! There were no tears when we drove away and all parties were upbeat and cheerful about it. Both had agreed to keep in touch when the opportunity presented itself. Together, they talked, laughed, and joked, until I dropped them off at the airport. I looked for signs of disappointment or sadness on the wife's face at that time but I couldn't see it. She had accepted her therapist's advice whole heartedly. I believed that the two of them were going to enjoy their time away, fully!

I laughed at myself when I acknowledged that it seemed I was more troubled about the situation than the rich couple were.

Rude Store Owner

*T*here was this Jewish lady who owned a convenience store a block or two from Glenwood Avenue and the Redwood Bridge. The place was set in an ideal location in that it was nestled amongst a densely populated area surrounded in dense bush, mostly oak trees. It was a beautiful setting. The store was attractive, inside and out. It was always well stocked and was pleasing to the eye. It was quaint but best of all it was the only store in the area. The area, as in, starting from Redwood Bridge, going all the way to Henderson Highway, up to Martin Avenue, then left to Glenwood Avenue and back to the Redwood Bridge. In all that area, hers was the only store, so she did a brisk business. For some reason, she didn't like me but I wasn't too offended. As it appeared to me, she didn't like or trust any cab driver. She lived in Garden City and she nagged me all the way to her store whenever I drove her there. Why did I turn at that street, slow down, go a little faster, why did you turn back there and why not at the other street? Slow down, speed up and so on.

This one morning when I dropped her off at her store, there was a small crowd of customers waiting for her to open. She had some items with her that she brought from her home and I helped her bring them in. Once inside the store I politely moved aside so as to allow her to serve her customers. I thought that because of that gesture, she would be appreciative. I was wrong! I waited patiently to get paid. Meanwhile, she chastised me to her customer saying I was ripping her off by taking her the long way to work. I refused to argue with her. When she saw that I wasn't going to engage myself in the conversation she abruptly stated that she wasn't going to pay me. "No problem," I said in a calm accepting voice and immediately started loading my arms with as many items that I could. In no time I had accumulated quite a valuable lot and started to walk out. In that short period of time I had amassed boxes of chocolate bars cakes, and even a display case of lighters, and a fistful of cigarettes. "Where are you going" she shrieked at me. Oh, I'll just take these items as payment for the ride, don't worry about it" I calmly stated. "Okay, Okay" she shouted. "I'll pay you!" and quickly opened her till to pay me. She threw a two dollar bill at me and ordered me out of her store. 'Thank you," I whispered. "It's been a pleasure doing business with you here today. You are always so pleasant to be around. I do hope you have an enjoyable day. And with that I dropped my arms to me sides, and all the items I had amassed, fell to the floor, then I turned to leave. "Pick those things up!" she ordered. I pretended that I didn't hear her and walked out the door "Have a great day I called over my shoulder". "Don't ever come into my store again," she called out after me. I kept quiet and continued walking. I walked out into the cold and never saw her again.

Closing Time

*O*ne of the most enticing elements that profoundly enhanced the taxi industry in the province of Manitoba was the liberal view the government took in its regulation of alcohol, in particular, how it regulated the bars and its hours of operation. Cabbies and the public loved the fact that all bars had to maintain a retail beer outlet. I was in awe as I would watch patrons stagger out of a bar at closing time so drunk that they literally could not stand, many on the verge of puking their guts out. Yet if someone who was even mildly inebriated tried to purchase liquor from a liquor store outlet, they would be refused. For bars, the times or hours of operation was a delight to cab drivers because they could make a lot of money picking up the many people off the street who hailed a cab, especially after the bars closed. On Monday, Tuesday, Wednesday, and Thursday, the bars closed at twelve thirty. On Friday and Saturday, they closed at one thirty in the morning and when that happened the scene all along Main Street transformed into a scene of Mardi-Gras like pandemonium. At closing time all the patrons spilled out onto the street, and because there were so many bars, there were a tremendous number of people lining the street. It looked like the crowds that line the street anxiously anticipating a Santa Clause parade. From Main Street to Selkirk there were hundreds of people under the influence meandering about. Most of them drunk, and all of them wanting a ride home! This is where taxi drivers cashed in by picking up these patrons and driving them home, which is what I did until five or six in the morning. I'd pick someone up, drive them home, then, head back down to Main Street for another fare. It was wild to say the least. There were fights or brawls going on everywhere, sometimes a stabbing or three. The people here were new to civilization having left the reserve for the first time. Many had never even seen a bus before. If an aboriginal man had an urge to pee, he simply unzipped himself and peed no matter where he stood. It was just the norm on the reservation. Some folks were engaged in sexual activities right there in full view of everyone, going at it against a wall. I remember watching a native man attempting to raise his case of beer and place it on a ledge over his head outside a window of the bar he had just emerged from. I saw a young woman, whom I thought was his sweetheart, start beating him. She landed a couple of punches but he wasn't as intoxicated as she may have thought because he recovered quickly and landed a few of his own, she went down hard and didn't get up again. At that moment a Duffy's taxi pulled up to the curb. The native left his predicament, moving his focus to the taxi. He quickly grabbed his case of beer pulling it down to his side which caused it to tear open letting out a few bottles to come crashing to the sidewalk. He left the broken glass bottles behind and scooped up the remainder and hopped into the waiting taxi. When I told my foreman, George he exclaimed in mockery, 'There is a God!" On busy nights like Friday and Saturday the paddy wagons moved up and down the streets like the trucks used to scoop up stray dogs. They spent their time collecting those passed out and lying on the sidewalk. The cops would then haul them off to the drunk tank. They would release them in the morning once they woke up. The scene was pitiful if not downright terrible. My heart was troubled by the whole scene.

Grand Theft Taxi

*W*ith all the driving we do, it's amazing that we don't have our cars stolen more often than what we do. The reason for that is because the vehicle is a marked car and it wouldn't take long for police to spot it and make arrests. Late one Friday afternoon l walked into the King's Hotel on Higgins to pick up a fare. As l walked through the door, four rowdy young men walked out. l didn't like the looks of them so l watched them closely. As soon as l spotted the group making a bee line for my cab, l stormed out after them. Unfortunately, l had gotten into the habit of leaving the keys in the ignition with the motor running, when going into a bar to get my fair. l did this for years with no problems. Not this time. In a flash they were gone. l ran back inside to let the bartender know that my car had been stolen. Three or four cop cars showed up in a matter of minutes. After a short chat they took off in pursuit after them, heading toward the Louise Bridge. l went along with them. The cops spotted the car a few blocks before the bridge. They quickly knocked on the door where an old lady answered and lied to the cops saying her boys weren't there, but they were. The cops ignored her and pushed passed her to apprehend the four young men. They threw the thieves into the squad car and drove them to jail. My cab was idling in the old lady's driveway. One cop said, "There's your cab pal!" I said "You mean I don't have to come down to the station and make out a report, a statement of incident and so on?" I was dreading the thought of having to spend hours and hours tied up on this theft thing, but, as it turned out, I didn't have to. I didn't ask any question. I quickly got into my car and drove away and continued my evening shift. It was a lesson well learned. I never again left my keys in my cars or left my cab idling.....not for a few months anyway!

Rainy Days and Mondays

For a while I worked day shift. Monday mornings are always the best time for lucrative airport trips because that's the time a lot of business men catch their fights to destinations everywhere in the country. Because of that, I usually began my day very early, on Monday mornings. I made it a point to be in my car, washed, gassed up, and out the garage door by 4am. The policy Red Patch Taxi had, as far as drivers work schedules were concerned, was that they didn't exist. Some mornings saw as little as 4 or 5 drivers, out of the whole fleet, show up before 9am. This policy often left the company temporarily, in dire straits.

One warm summer Monday morning I arrived at the office anxious to get started. I was expecting an above average day as the conditions were perfect. It was raining buckets. I was right on time, 4am, and so. I was determined to get an early start. Also, there were a lot of booked trips on the dispatcher's table that morning when I arrived at work. Besides, the phones were ringing off the hook, yet there were only four cars on the road at the time, counting me. I knew I could run off 5 or 6 airport trips by 9 am which would, by itself, make my day. After that, as they say, the rest is gravy. When I got to the garage to retrieve my car, the dispatcher was in panic mode and told me to forget washing the car and chased me off to Transcona to pick up my first trip of the day. I was delighted because this meant I would start my day with a $14.00 trip or more which was, a great way to start. I noticed that the water on the streets were level with the curb. There were no sign of the rain letting up, and, judging by the look of panic on the dispatcher's face, and, the strain in his voice when he chased me out of the garage, told me that this fare was not going to be a happy camper. He couldn't have over exaggerated the situation more. When I pulled into his driveway a gentleman in a light weight coat stood, impervious to the pouring rain. I noticed the garage door closing behind him. I didn't realize that he wasn't being a Spartan by standing there; it was because he was seething with rage. He was holding 2 pieces of luggage. The second I came to a stop the gentleman flashed past my window, opened my back door then violently threw in his luggage. He then streaked to the passenger seat, before I had a chance to bring my cab to a full stop. I quickly put the car in reverse which, apparently, was the signal for the verbal abuse to begin. I looked over at his face which was dripping heavily with rain. "Move, move, move," he roared "let's get this piece of shit going I have a flight to catch which I will probably miss, because you decided to eat a couple donuts at Timmy's this morning before getting your lazy ass on the job!" My first instinct was to pull over and physically throw him and his luggage, out on the street. "You were supposed to be here an hour and ten minutes ago! Were you hustling some hot chick somewhere on the parking lot? I called ten times and you get here now!" He roared incredulously loud, mixed together with personal insults and a few foul curse words as well. It was then that I slammed on the brakes causing us both the hit the dash. This time I was doing the roaring. "Do you see a phone anywhere on the dash in this car?! You never called or spoke to me, so I don't know how long you've been waiting! I don't care how many times you called! I never got you your call, period. My dispatcher gave me your call the second I got to my office, ten minutes ago! I had no time for a coffee, no time to wash my car, or take a piss. The entire ten minutes were spent driving here so I could pick you up and drive you to the airport!" When I had finished my own rant, there was a lull in the air. It took a few seconds before the fare realized we were stopped. He roared again. It was as if he hadn't heard a word I had said. "Move" He screamed. "I've got a plane to catch!" My own little tirade had put his abuse to rest but he was still highly agitated. He rocked back and forth in his seat letting out a litany of foul curse words under his breath all the while as I drove along. I drove as fast

266

as I could with my eye out for cops who might have been out manning their radar traps. I could hear the water plashing hard under the undercarriage of the car and I started to worry about the possibility of stalling. Sure enough, as I was sailing with good speed down St. James Street, I hit a huge puddle when the car stalled. Because of his maniacal reaction, I thought the guy was going to suffer a heart attack. It was comical to watch him waving his arms frantically about and moving forward and backward like a beaver caught in a leg-hold trap. His head spasmodically moved from one side to another disbelieving what he was seeing. We weren't moving! With exaggerating gestures with his hands, his voice took on the tone of a man condemned to the gallows. His eyes bulged out of his head and he again roared, "Let's go, start it up! Let's go! Let's go" A great calm came over me because I was starting to enjoy this. In a calm controlled voice I said, "It's still raining cats and dogs out there and as you can see, the water on the street is level with the curb and it's not letting up. The distributer cap is wet which means we must wait a few minutes for it to dry out." This part of the entire trip was the hardest part for him to take. I waited about 5 minutes and turned the key. Alleluia, it started. This time I drove slowly, careful not to hasten through the curb high puddles. The fare didn't take this well. "I'm going to sue you when I get back!" he threatened. "I'll own this crappy taxi business just so I can fire you! I'm going to sue Chuck too. He'll be penniless when I get through with him!" He raved on as I carried on at 25 miles an hour. Finally, I pulled up to the terminal doors where he bounded out in a flash. He fished out a $50 bill and threw it at me. The bill landed on the seat next to me and I quickly scooped it up. This time it was I who yelled at him. "I don't have change for a fifty dollar bill at five o'clock in the morning. What do you think I am, a bank? I held the bill tight in my fist with no intention of letting it go. I continued, "Wait inside and I'll have security come down and take a statement and write up a report so you won't lose any cash. It shouldn't take more than an hour. I'm sure the pilot will wait." He cursed out loud and slammed the door so hard that I thought the windows were going to shatter. He was still cursing as he disappeared through the terminal doors running at a full gallop. Neither Chuck nor I got sued. What a tip I thought. The abuse and entertainment of it all was worth it.

Taxi Durability

ed Patch Taxi had thirty three cars. When it came to replacing the older cars, Chuck, the owner, had a simple system. Every year he would buy eleven brand new vehicles which happened to be General Motors Chevrolet Biscayne's. They were the ones that replaced the eleven oldest cars in the fleet. One day after my first year of working at Red Patch Taxi, 1 came to work one morning to find a few new faces, new mechanics, donning white G.M. smocks, working on our oldest cars. Apparently, or so 1 was told, this was not so unusual. They did all their testing on these cars, even sawing the engine block in half and measuring for wear and tear. 1 figured that had to be substantial. Not so, the tech guy told me. In fact there was zero wear and tear on the motors. 1 was stunned to hear that. When I questioned how that was possible, 1 was told it was because of the continuous running of taxi cabs over the tree year period that they were in use. Apparently it's the continuous stop and go that wear out the engine, in regular vehicles. I know we went through a lot of other parts over the years like transmissions; all kinds of bearings and stuff but the motors were virtually untouched.

I know that in the winter, drivers often got themselves stuck in snow. Being too anxious to wait for a tow truck, a driver would drive forward then reverse, back and forth, until they had managed to sometimes, get out. The down side to that maneuver was that it burned out the transmission, in which case Chuck took it out of the drivers pay check. That usually added up to about three hundred and fifty dollars way back when. And he didn't ask he just took it. The same went for any reason a tow truck was needed. You got stuck in a snow drift or anywhere else, you paid.

In Hot Persuit

There are many sights a cab driver witnesses almost on a daily basis and while most of them mean nothing significant but they do offer up a glimpse of what might have been. One late Thursday night, or was it early Friday morning? I don't remember exactly anymore. It was around three in the morning when I dropped off my fare on St. James Street. I was driving down Portage Avenue heading back home. I had arrived at the Army Navy Surplus store, a stone's throw away from the Hudson Bay Store. I had just passed the University of Winnipeg and closing in on the Army Navy Surplus Store, when a short white young man with a dark beard came running out of the shadows. He was running for all he was worth! As a matter of fact, I can say with certainty, that I had never seen anyone run so fast, unless they were competing for an Olympic gold medal. He was running so fast that the heels of his shoes were hitting his butt with every swift step. Both his arms moved in perfect Unison like an experienced well trained athlete. He had the most intense look of desperation on his face as if a hit squad were in hot pursuit. He ran in a perfectly straight line, attempting to cover the shortest distance possible in the shortest amount of time possible. He cut across four lanes of traffic, moving in a perfectly diagonal line which ended by the West wall of the University of Winnipeg. He quickly covered that distance, which I estimated to be at least a hundred yards. He soon disappeared between two houses which I knew from experience, would take him to a laneway and then to Ellis Avenue. The scene only lasted one minute, but I knew more was going to follow. Sure enough something did. I had pulled over to the curb from where I first saw the sprinter emerge in my peripheral vision. Then I waited. Just as the runner disappeared from view, a cop, with his gun drawn, came out of the same shadows where the runner had emerged from earlier. Soon, a second cop, with his gun drawn emerged. While the two cops took a few seconds to catch their breath, their eyes searched frantically for their perpetrator, but it was in vain, he got away. What he got away with, or from whom, I had no idea, but he looked clean-cut. I saw no weapon in his hands, or blood on his person, so, I determined that he wasn't likely a victim or a perpetrator, therefore; I had no desire to interfere. I already had a job.

Mystery Man Fatality

Some sights that I have witnessed as a cab driver have remained a mystery to me. By that, I mean that after seeing bizarre scenes of violence or depravity, yet many of them never appeared on TV or in a newspaper. For example I remember one Wednesday in the wee small hours of the morning I was driving over the Louise Bridge. When I had passed Sutherland Avenue I heard the loud continuous alarm ringing near one of the flour mills on Sutherland. Those bells had been blaring away for the last 5 hours but there were no cop cars parked anywhere and no police presence anywhere. But now as I continued down Higgins Avenue toward Main Street somewhere in the vicinity, other alarms were going off. During those hours I had relayed many fares from Elmwood and East Kildonan to downtown. It was always normal on any given night to do so. All the while, as I drove back and forth via Sutherland and, or, Higgins those alarms never stopped ringing. Whatever I thought might be going down, was pure speculation on my part. I knew whatever it might be, it was not good. The scene was anti climatic to say the least. It was simply an eerily quiet night.

Finally around 3 am, as I was driving a late street fare home over the Louise bridge I saw the bloody explanation of all this mayhem going on where Sutherland meets Higgins at the bridge. If you are driving west over the Louise bridge you can continue to main street or, almost immediately emerging from the bridge, you can turn right on Sutherland and eventually hit north Main street. The intersection takes on the shape of a perfect triangle. There, lying in the right lane as you exit off Sutherland onto Higgins, a large fifty year old looking man lay flat on his back, blood drained from his head in what looked like a gun injury. The blood trickled down the asphalt, accumulating at the lowest point at the bottom of Higgins, one hundred and fifty feet from the Louise Bridge. The big man was face up with a bullet hole in the middle of his forehead. Just viewing the crooked line of blood on the road from the back of this man's head, made me think of a page out of a Stephen King novel. The man, whoever he was, was obviously dead. To this day, I can only guess what might have taken place. Looking at the scene at face value, It looked like a robbery gone bad and the cops used cold, deadly force to resolve the situation. I never heard a word about it on the radio or television and certainly, nothing of it in any newspaper.

Cop or Mass Murderer?

*T*his event didn't happen to me, it happened to my wife Patricia who drove for the same company that I did (Red Patch Taxi). She usually worked days and I mostly worked nights where things were, at times, more challenging. This one day my wife was asked to take a crew of engineers to Portage La Prairie in order to take control of a train and transport it to some other destination. The three man crew and my wife left Symington Diesel Shop and headed out. My wife and I both knew that some taxi experiences can be nerve shattering, scary, and sometimes downright dangerous. It was a normal run on a normal, quiet, beautiful summer afternoon. The driving conditions were perfect, as there was no rain and visibility was 100%. The extensive view of wheat fields could be seen clearly on both sides of the highway. My wife said they were all interacting in calm easy conversation when she said she noticed something in the middle of the road a long distance away. "It was really just a dot on the horizon on the highway. She asked the crew what they thought it might be; which quickly caught their interest. She lowered her speed, and kept moving slowly until they could see that there was a mysterious figure. There, in the middle of the road was a man in uniform with a rifle held in a shooters stance with his rifle aimed at her car. She came to a full stop and immediately, he approached the driver's door with his gun aimed at her head with great agitation and aggression. He didn't identify himself but screamed at her to get out of the car. Everyone in the car including the three crew men became un-nerved. One man in the back seat told my wife not to stop, but to keep going. Which, if she would have, this psycho cop impersonator would have surely shot her dead. He continued to yell at her, ordering her to get out of her car. My wife refused to move and said. "No!" finally he asked my wife if she knew how fast she was going and my wife answered a resounding yes! 'I was going fifty five miles an hour, give or take a few miles." He scoffed at her and screamed at her accusing her of going one hundred and ten miles an hour, at which, my wife scoffed. That had to be the most absurd statement anyone had ever accused my wife of doing. All three members of the crew scoffed at this guy's accusation as well and even mentioned that they would happily appear on my wife's behalf to testify in court if it ever came to that. Amid this fabrication of lies my wife picked up her microphone and called the dispatcher and said, "I've got a situation here, I need the 10-7s!" The dispatcher answered and asked what her problem was. It was at this point that that this man in uniform said, "I'll let you go with a warning, this time, but I will be watching for you." My wife said she had the tremors so bad that she had a hard time to drive after that. She was in tears. Even as she drove away this psycho cop still had the rifle trained on her car. As she drove shakily away the crew gave their own observations. One crew member quipped, "Whoever that guy was he didn't have a radar gun." Another added, "Where's his patrol car anyway?" It was this statement that made everyone look around but there was no sign of a police car anywhere to be seen. What scared my wife the most was the fact that she had to return on the same route to get back to Winnipeg by herself. She would not even have had anyone to support her. She called the office and told them what happened and they said to keep the mike real close to her. As it turned out, the guy was nowhere to be seen, to her great relief. This happened nearly forty years ago and my wife still shivers when she thinks about it. This story reminds me of a Stephen King story called Cops. I doubt very much if that whack job was a cop, but if he was one, he shouldn't have been one. Pointing a rifle at the head of a woman and ordering her out of the cab, for speeding, which she wasn't doing, wreaks of something ominous and threatening, if not downright scary. The guy's either a psychopath or a mass murderer. Who knows!? I wonder how many citizens got pulled over by the fool. I would be interested to hear from anyone if they did.

Don't get me wrong, here I have the deepest respect for police officers and I don't envy their jobs, I've seen what they go through at times. But, it only takes one psycho to destroy the trust and reputation of the entire force.

Self Incriminating Witness

innipeg is especially beautiful in the summer. It can be exciting to take a joy ride up and down the strip with your significant other or just good friends, on a nice warm summer evening. On such a night, drivers cruise along with their windows down where the rock and pop music pours out through the open windows. Young lovers cruise around, frequenting places like, Salisbury House, A&W, or Kelekis' restaurant, to name but a few of some of their favorite places to gather and socialize, making lifelong memories. I was enjoying my night shift on this one particular Friday evening as I was returning from dropping off a fare near Inkster and Salter. I was slowly making my way down Main Street, heading south toward City Hall, just savoring the evening. The warm breeze, the good music, the peaceful flow of traffic was intoxicating. It was only a few minutes past nine as I drove by Kelekis' restaurant when I caught the savory whiff of burger and fries. I decided right then and there to stop in and pick up some food. I had often eaten there before as it was definitely one of my favorite places to eat.

I found their food the best in the city, especially their fresh cut fries, which I declare to be the tastiest in all of Canada. I pulled over to the curb just past the restaurant and went inside to place my order. Later, I walked out with my meal of burger and fries heading back to my waiting taxi. Once inside I started in on my delicious feast. My lunch was suddenly interrupted by the deafening sound of a car roaring from somewhere in the direction behind me, accompanied with the sound of tires screeching over the pavement. I stretched my neck toward the sound that as near as I could tell, was coming from the area of the Redwood Bridge. Whatever it was, it was coming my way, and quickly. I couldn't even guess how fast he was moving but I cringed, expecting something disastrous to happen any second.

The driver, in his ever increasing speed, wrestled for control of the steering wheel as he tried to navigate his sharp turn onto Main Street. He overcompensated; sending him on the left side of the cement divider facing a mass of oncoming north bound vehicles. In his desperation, he tried to maneuver over the barricade, all the while accelerating as fast as it was possible for a car to accelerate, he realized he needed to be on the west side of the divider so that he would end up in the southbound lane. Because the divider was too high, the car flipped onto its roof and continued upside down for half a block, spewing a steady stream of brilliant sparks until it came to rest in the middle lane of south bound traffic. The horn was left blaring and the light were on.

I quickly tossed the remainder of my dinner over to the passenger side of the front seat and rushed out to see if I could be of help. When I reached the wreck, hundreds of people had gathered there already. I couldn't figure how so many people had showed up so quickly. The first thing I noticed was that the vehicle was a souped up 1941 Mercury Monarch. Colorful flames had been painted on both sides of the car. There was chrome everywhere, both bumpers, wheels, and under the hood, which I could clearly see because the hood had been torn away from the car, leaving everything under the hood, exposed.

I soon heard the wail of sirens and in no time cops were swarming everywhere at the scene. They quickly set up barriers, separating the wreck from the on-lookers. As near as I could tell, there were no dead or mutilated bodies lying around. I was standing on the curb just over one of the barricades with a cop standing right in front of me, but ignoring me. The mob of people at the scene seemed as curious as I was as to who the moron was who drove like an idiot to cause this much chaos. The crowd was abuzz with chatter. The police looked mystified, probably wondering the same thing everyone else was, were was the driver? The car was completely empty. Suddenly, I caught the movement of a tall skinny man staggering my way from across the east side of the street. He struggled to stay upright and I marveled that he could manage to make it to this side of the road. When he finally reached the cop who was in front of me, he lost his balance and fell onto the cop's arm, hugging him aggressively in order not to fall. The officer reached out, grabbing him by the shoulders in order to steady him. The man was as drunk as a man could be without passing out, which explained why he had such difficulty standing, plus, his speech was so slurred, that neither the cop nor I, could understand a word he said. Finally the drunk spoke something that we could understand. "What the hell happened?" He asked in desperation, slobbering profusely as he talked. The officer simply said, "Sir, stay on that side of the barrier, this is an ongoing investigation!" Ignoring the police officer's instructions, the drunk repeated his question. "What the hell happened?" with his voice, highly stressed and anxious. I could see the frustration etched on the cop's face and I figured he was ready to physically remove this annoying rubber neck pedestrian. The officer repeated the instruction he had instructed earlier but again the drunk repeated his, "What the hell happened?" he inquired. The cop finally looked the man in the face and asked, "Who the hell are you?" Without hesitation, the drunk in his most frantic and desperate voice loudly proclaimed, looking the cop in the eye and pointing to the mangled wreck in front of us said, "I'm the driver, and that's my car!!" Without speaking another word, the police officer wrestled the drunk to the ground, slipped the cuffs on him, called a couple other officers and carried him away. I made it back to my cab but I couldn't finish my supper, I was laughing too much.

Restless Runaway

eenagers are hard on parents from time to time, especially when the bonds of attachment are challenged. After every school year in Winnipeg, celebrations for kids, fresh out of high school, start. It becomes even more pronounced for high school graduates. Some have been waiting years to spread their wings and it often results in confrontation and outright family war. Unfortunately for me, I happened upon such a scene. It was Saturday June 30 just past two o'clock in the afternoon. I was dispatched to a beautiful home on Edison Avenue in North Kildonan. It was a bright sunny summer day and when I pulled into the driveway everything seemed serene and quite normal. The only thing odd, which I didn't catch at the time, was a teen who approached me from the side of the house, dressed as if she were ready to hit the road. She had a stuffed back pack strapped to her back and what looked like a large overnight bag in her hand. She wore a beige wool knit sweater which I felt was too warm for the weather.

She also wore a tight pair of denim jeans and a matching denim jacket. I felt a heat wave pass over me just looking at her and wondered where on earth was she going dressed like that? I opened the back door and she said, "The Ex!" even before I asked her where she was going. Every year at the end of the school year, the Red River Exhibition, which was a very large mid way set up just past Polo Park down Portage Avenue. It was just referred to as 'The Ex'.

As if on cue, after the young lady gave me her destination, her mother sprang like a gazelle from the garage as if she were being chased by lions. The mother was hysterical and exploded into tears, ordering her daughter out of my taxi. In a flash the mother reached the back door of the cab screaming and yelling and managed to swing the door wide open, which immediately prompted me to shut off the Motor and place the car in park. I knew I wasn't going anywhere for the moment so I thought it best to see how this was going to play itself out. Both parties did a lot of hysterical demands and accusations with neither side gaining any ground.

The spectacle continued in their driveway which soon drew a crowd of neighbors and passersby who quietly congregated near the centre of chaos and forming a circle around the combatants. I felt like the ringmaster of a three ring circus. I didn't want the attention, I was embarrassed so I slinked down behind my steering wheel as far as I could, hoping to stay ignored. In desperation, the mother turned to me and demanded that I throw the teen out of my car and drive away. When I told her it was none of my business she threatened me with a lawsuit and called me a criminal because I was abducting her daughter against her (the mother's) will. The bickering continued and I was relieved when the cops showed up.

The police questioned me and I quickly relayed my part on the scene. The senior officer marched up to the distraught mother and took effective charge of the situation. "Ma'am." He said. Get hold of yourself and tell me what's going on here." The other officer took care of the onlookers and told them to mind their own business and move along. Once the small crowd was gone, the mother spoke, through tears. She explained through sniffs and sobs that her daughter had just graduated from high school that summer. She had been an honor student all through high school and had always talked of being a veterinarian someday. But lately she only talked about leaving home to travel the world.

The mother felt that her daughter was too young and inexperienced to hit the road. When the daughter exited the cab the mother became combative and attempted to wrestle the back pack from her daughter's hand, but she wasn't stronger than her daughter and the officer had to interfere. The daughter then let out a litany of curse words at her mother, at which point the officer put a stop to the whole thing.

Finally the officer asked mom how old her daughter was. Nineteen! She screamed. I'm not sure what else was said because by this time I just wanted to drive away, with or without a fare. I did stay long enough to hear the officer say that the daughter was an adult and had the right to leave and try to work things out sometime in the future. With that confirmation the daughter slipped back into the back seat and slammed her door. I quickly started up my car and drove slowly away. The last thing I saw in my rear view mirror was the mother sobbing uncontrollably as she hugged the officer and the other officer patting her on the back. I don't know exactly what was being said but I got the gist of it all. I wasn't a parent at that time but I thought if I ever have children some day, and some of them are girls, I hope I live on an island!

The Cretin Of Point Douglas

*T*here was a period of time in the 1970's when a lot of press was given about the chronic abuse of alcohol that was rampant amongst the native population in Manitoba. It seemed nowhere was it more visible than on the streets of our fair city. The public was shocked to learn, through the various media venues, just what sort of liquids alcoholics drink to become intoxicated. Things like shaving lotion, shoe polish, vanilla extract, and Lysol to name a few. I was sometimes bemused whenever a group of men staggered into my car so drunk and disheveled that they couldn't stand and were of slurred speech. They looked terrible yet they smelled like a million bucks. It was the only manifestation of civility about them. I remember reading about people being hospitalized because they had consumed Lysol or imitation vanilla extract and so on, to the point that the media put pressure on the public to not have confectionary outlets sell these items at all, thus eliminating possible access to the most vulnerable. It seems that there was a continuous campaign to clean things up, yet tragic fatal stories of alcohol and drug abuse kept appearing in our newspapers. It was a real struggle but the media and the politicians united influences to promote awareness of this problem and the positive measures to fight it. For the longest time the public became aware of the war on the abuse situation and soon most corner stores stopped stocking and selling the substances mentioned in this story. It looked like the campaign was working because it became hard to find Lysol or shoe polish from any local outlet. If a man went into a store to buy more than one bottle of aftershave it raised the suspicions of the pharmacist. It was easier for a young man to buy cigarettes. So, by and large, it looked like the battle was beginning to yield some signs of victory and even the public at large were supporting the struggle.

One dreary Sunday morning I had just dropped off a fare and I was negotiating my way back to Redwood bridge area. I spotted an old dilapidated confectionary store almost hidden among the surrounding nondescript houses. I suddenly had an urge to buy a Pepsi so I stepped into the place to make my purchase. It was a drab old place that looked deserted and I had to squint my eyes when I first walked in because the lights were so dim.

There was a pop cooler at the far end of the room. There were about five or six empty shelves that ran the entire length of the wall behind the counter. The only items I spied on the shelves were bottles and bottles of Lysol. There had to be hundreds of them. I was surprised that he had pop for sale. He didn't have bread or milk for sale, or the odd can of beans or soup. The message boomed into my brain like a shock wave. I gasped in amazement when the reality of the scene set in. A tiny bespectacled East Indian man stood silently behind the counter watching me. Here it was, a time when the media and the politicians were finally working together to fight alcohol abuse, that was so prevalent amongst young people and natives in particular, because that was who, most of all, this press was targeting. Here was a man, who was doing his best to capitalize on the problem. I was mad at this little cretin for being so callous and indifferent to the affected masses. I felt like breaking every bottle on his shelves. He stood by his cash register with his hand out ready to receive my money. I said. "You're really a scumbag you know, people are dying, losing their lives and destroying their families, and here you are, indifferent by selling this poison and helping to destroy people and lives. You're only concerned about making money." I was so angry. I put my hand back into my pocket. I was boiling mad when I said with a clenched jaw, "You're a cretin and I wish you would go back to wherever it is you come from!" "You are nothing but a scourge to my country! I'm not paying you for this Pepsi, but feel free to attack me or to call the cops because I'm sure they would love to see what you're doing here in this hole. I'm sure the newspaper would love to take your picture and print your story. You can bet people will stop coming to your store! I know I'm never coming back!" With that said I walked out with my Pepsi, still incensed about this immigrant's callous disregard and reckless endangerment for his fellow man. I called a newspaper a short time after and told them there could be a good story at that establishment but I never heard anything about it on the news. I believe that by doing nothing when we witness an atrocity like this, sometimes we can be part of the problem.

Red Patch Weasel

There was a young man who worked for Red Patch Taxi at that time, in the 1970's, whom I nick named the weasel. Sometimes, I playfully called him Wally the Weasel or just Wally, for short. But, most often, I referred to him as the weasel, like I'm doing now in this book. He was above average in intelligence, which made him all the more despicable. He knew the city like the back of his hand and never forgot an address. When he wasn't dispatching, he was driving. While he was driving, he paid close attention to what was going on over his radio. He capitalized on whatever information was coming over the air and when an opportunity came up, he didn't hesitate to seize it. He was fast and he was unscrupulous when it came to scooping another driver's fare. He was very good at it! Because of his unethical proficiency in the trade and how skilled he was as a driver, he made the rest of us look like, 'a monkey's uncle,' as the saying goes. He was a prolific hustler. In most cases, new drivers were inherently nervous and consequently, they often took longer to get to their given address. Upon hearing a rookie driver stammering and stuttering and exhibiting other nervous characteristics over the air, like getting lost, the weasel would make a bee line to that address and scoop the fare from right under his or her nose. By the time the dispatcher got the newbie to the right address, it was too late. The weasel was already counting his money. Another thing he did as a dispatcher was to 'feed' his buddies. So that means when a good trip would come in, he would tell one of his cronies over the radio to call him or come in to the office. He then would give them the trip without it going over the air so the other drivers did not know about it.

Unfortunately, for the company, the weasel ended up on the night shift which opened another door through which he could capitalize on a new rip off venture and line his pockets with even more money than before. In front of the office were a set of gas pumps which were for the drivers to fill up their taxis at the end of their shifts.

He started selling gas to the drivers from the company's gas pump. He would allow the drivers to gas up, their personal vehicles at the company's gas pumps for a nominal fee. Chuck was nobody's fool. It didn't take long for him to realize what was going on. There used to be a brick yard behind a chain link fence just a stone's throw away from the Red Patch Garage. Nobody noticed when, what looked like an outhouse, suddenly went up conspicuously close to the edge of the steel fence, facing the company's gas pumps. Everything was caught on video. It showed driver after driver gassing up at the pumps after work and slipping a few bucks to the weasel as a payoff. A couple times I was tempted to take advantage of the cheap gas but thought better of it. The Red Patch Weasel was not a big guy and certainly no match for the fury Chuck was certain to unleash on him, once the damning evidence fell into his hands. I wish I could have been there when the crap hit the fan. Like a lot of other drivers, I was often a victim of his thieving ways when I was new. So I wasn't overly fond of him. However I did get an account of the event when it went down in the office. The Manager of the company at the time, gave me the lowdown, and according to him, it went like this: Chuck, a big man with strong rugged features calmly and politely called the Weasel into his office. He told the hapless dispatcher to sit down. From this point on, I'll use the name ghost interchangeably because, in another era, when Chuck was sending his bad drivers to the hospital in droves, I imagine, that under this particular circumstance, he might have sent this character, to the morgue. I'm sure when the ghost was confronted; he envisioned his life coming to a painful end. But, Chuck knew if he laid a severe beating on the weasel, the weasel would have been intelligent enough to consult a lawyer and launch a seven digit lawsuit. The ghost sat nervously across from Chuck's desk, sweating bullets, wondering what was about to go down. Chuck

294

calmly opened a thick manila envelope and tossed a stack of 8 1/2 by 11, high gloss color photographs of drivers gassing up at his gas pump, and the passing of cash to the weasel. The weasel's face instantly turned white. Before he could speak a word, chuck ran from behind his desk and, placed both of his massive hands around the weasel's neck and lifted him right out of the chair. His feet dangled like a puppet as chuck smashed him against the wall. With one hand pinning the thief against the wall, Chuck roared in his face and basically told him that if he wanted to avoid a lengthy and painful hospital stay, he would sign legal documents prepared by his expensive lawyers that damned him, if, and in case, Chuck ever wanted to use it against him anytime in the future. It was meant mostly to be used against him, if any of the thief's prospective employers ever contacted him for a reference. Chuck calculated that approximately $3000 in fuel was stolen and he expected the weasel to pay every dime of it back. If he didn't, then the damning document would be used to make his life very miserable. He agreed to all the terms in the document of course and signed it. Finally, the weasel walked out of Chuck's office on wobbly legs, anxious about what he had signed but greatly relieved that he was still upright with no scars covering his face and body. I figure the weasel got off easy. I thought a few scars, bumps, and bruises would have been an appropriate send off, but that was just my opinion.

Temptation

You meet a lot of rough characters when you drive a taxi. If you wanted to hire a guy to murder someone, you could find them as one of your passengers. Or, if you wanted to get into the counterfeiting game, you could find somebody for that too. Anything! One thing I found about these shady ex-cons was that they were filled with confidence, misdirected though it was. It seems that the opportunity to commit crime excited them, much like a used car salesman is overcome with when he spots a potential client peering through a vehicle's driver window. Sadly that energy can get passed on to others making them momentarily, lose touch with reality.

I remember meeting this personable shady character who told me he knew someone who would happily kill an enemy of mine for as low as seventy five bucks. Then he told me that he knew this guy who was hired to kill someone. He stalked his prey and finally shot him when he was making a call from a phone booth somewhere on some street corner. I kind of think he was trying to impress me, but Winnipeg North-enders, maybe not. They could be real rough necks.

Whatever kind of a crime you want done, I guarantee you, it wouldn't take long to find him or her. Often people propositioned me, trying to entice me to purchase stolen goods. One such character pressured me for the job. "Whatever you want, he said, I can get it for you." he pleaded. He even asked me what size I took for a high end leather coat. I felt like I was ordering merchandise from Eaton's order desk. Anything I wanted, in any size or color, and he guaranteed delivery faster than the department stores. The offers were plenty and sometimes tempting but I had a perfectly clean record, and still have. However profitable a score might yield, my father told me it was never worth ruining your family name over. Good sound advice which I've always adhered to and passed on to my children. You meet a lot of characters who are good at committing a slew of crimes but I tended to stay away from them. I listen to them talk and say "Oh ya? Uh huh. Sure. Etc. etc. But that was as far as it went.

Once, I flirted with crime. Which scared the pants off me but, luckily I salvaged that before it got too far.

Case in point: One evening I met this man who had recently been released from prison for committing arson. I was intrigued with his story because I had purchased my first home a number of years earlier and I realized that if my house burned down, I would receive a tidy sum. It was kind of like when someone buys life insurance and you joke how rich you would feel if that person accidently died or was pushed off a building. You joke about it but you know you would feel bad if that family member actually did meet this fate. As part of the conversation I said, "I should hire you to burn my house down and then I could collect the insurance. Then I could pay off my mortgage and still would have enough money left over to buy a more expensive home. Of course it would have to look accidental. The guy instantly picked up on this idea with much enthusiasm. He said that for a thousand dollars he knew how to fix up my tv to make it look totally accidental and untraceable. I knew instantly that I had dug myself a hole, because this guy was already hyperventilating. I instantly wanted to get rid of this guy as fast as possible but I figured he could become violent if I said I was only joking. I knew I had stepped over the line in this insane potential misadventure. My heart was beating like a drum. I knew I had to shake this guy and quickly and as tactfully as possible without upsetting him. I pretended that I wanted to hire him. I arranged for us to meet the next day at the Ponderosa restaurant on Henderson Highway and Springfield Road. I told him I would buy him lunch and we could go over the details afterwards. He shook my hand when he got out of my cab. I felt a great deal of relief when he waved good-by. I never showed up. I also never allowed myself to be drawn into potentially dangerous conversations again. I beat

298

myself up for that stupid idea for a long time and vowed, never again!

I'll just stick to fantasizing about collecting someone's million dollar insurance policy. At least we can both laugh and joke about it. My warped sense of humor almost did me in.

Long Distance teen
Tramp Learns Con

S peaking of cops, the biggest lesson I learned was not to depend on them. Like the time when the cop said it was my word against my thief's word. This cancelled everything out as he staggered away with a wide smirk on his inebriated face. I'd been had. I was surprised the cop didn't light up the guy's cigarette, pat him on his scrawny back, shake his hand, and enthusiastically wave him good-by, as they slinked back in their cruiser, rushing to the nearest Tim Horton's. I learned to handle things myself and that even if it meant, rolling in the dirt, so be it. Forget was my motto. Even well intentioned or well meaning cops were uncaring and ineffective. This was brought home to me one early winter evening in Transcona. I had sat for almost an hour and a half sitting in my cab in front of the Regent hotel in Transcona. For most of that time I observed an adult man whom I figured to be in his early thirties, standing with a young female teenager, whom I figured to be fourteen at the most. Most of the time that I sat there, these two people had stood outside the bar enduring the cold and steady onslaught of freezing rain. Finally the adult said something to the girl, I believe it was a final word of instruction before he quickly stepped away leaving the girl alone outside the bar doors. Immediately, she walked to my car and got herself in. She gave me an address in Fort Gary and quietly settled into her seat. The freezing rain soon turned to snow so that by the time I arrived at her destination the world was covered with fresh fallen snow. It made the world there appear like a Trish Romance painting. When I came to a stop, the teen said, "I have to run inside to get the money from my mom so you will hear the door slam when she come out to bring you the money, she should be out in only a minute of two. This was still in my early driving career and I was still naïve, still not housebroken.

I knew she had to be close by, at least close enough to hear a door slam. I thought that because of her statement, I had nothing to worry about. It turns out I had something to worry about after all. The dispatcher sent the cops out, but this time it only took an hour and ten minutes for them to get there, unlike the three and a half hours the first time the cops were summoned. It was still snowing when the police showed up and I went over everything with them including the part with the slamming door. Thanks to the new fallen snow the senior officer traced the teen's tracks right to her door, but it took some time to do it. As all three of us huddled underneath the stoop I took a closer look at the two officers. The senior police officer was older, probably late thirties, early forties, hence more professional. It was he who led the way while the three off us followed. He tracked the girl's footprints right to her door. He knocked on the door and spoke with the mother, who expressed deep shame and anger when she found out that her daughter was in the company with this undesirable much older male adult. It turns out the mother had no cash which means I had to make arrangements to come back a week later and set a time to pick up my money. It was way too much effort for the money. The younger officer looked like a great big goof, that this was probably, his first gig. He couldn't have been more than twenty years of age, and I guessed that he was the son of a cop who was on the force who managed to influence someone higher up the food chain to hire him. I doubted he had started shaving yet. What really got me was the stupid smirk on his face. It looked like he thought this was really neat. I imagined him chuckling in a deep voice like Goofy. "Hyuk, hyuk, ever neat!!, "Hyuk Hyuk." It was then and there I decided from now on I would never, under any circumstance, call a cop again. I never did.

Meter Phobia

*A*ny cabbie who thinks they can make more money by keeping you longer in their taxi either by taking the long way around or making wrong turns and so on is a fool. Nothing could be further from the truth. The only one getting ripped off is the driver. Why, you ask? The answer is simple. The sooner the driver gets you to your destination, the sooner he or she is free and open for another fare. Many drivers will refuse out of town trips for this very reason. The time it takes a driver to run off an out of town trip is often less than if that same driver had stayed in town and ran off a slew of shorter trips and earned more money, sometimes 50% more! And that's not counting the tips you lose. At the time that I drove cab in Winnipeg, the meters started at fifty five cents and it dropped a dime every so many kilometers. But the way most people reacted if I missed a turn, you would have thought that I had pistoled whipped and bludgeoned them out of their life savings. I once worked for a rival taxi company that offered seniors a 10% discount off their fares. Some seniors, whose fare turned out to be as little as seventy five cents, demanded the discount. I understand the plight some seniors live under, but I felt the company should pay that discount off their ledger and not off the cab driver's tally sheet. I remember picking up a lady at her hair salon and drove her to her new expensive home in North Kildonan. Her fare ran $3.25. When she asked for her senior's discount I asked her how much she paid for her perm. She answered $75.00. I then asked her how much of a discount her hair dresser knocked off her perm. She scoffed and said, "nothing, she does a wonderful job!" I said, "I do a wonderful job too. I drive you safely to and from your destination, I open your doors when you enter and when you leave my cab, which is always kept clean and smelling fresh. I obey all the rules of the road and make it my business to drive in complete safety. I don't expect a tip nor do I give a discount. If my company wants to give you a discount, call them and tell them you think they should give you one. As long as it doesn't come off my paycheck, I couldn't care less." I left it at that and soon switched companies.

Moving On Out

*O*ne beautiful day in late June, I picked up a C.N. employee at the train depot and helped him load his baggage into the trunk of my car. Before he got into the taxi he went into a phone booth and made a call. He was a young man of about twenty six or seven and he told me that he worked on a work gang with C.N. Rail, which meant he was out of town for weeks at a time. As it was, he had been gone for three weeks and he was looking forward to getting home again. He told me that he had presently had a woman living with him but he was determined to change that situation as soon as he got home. He knew that she had been partying every night of the week when he was away. Without really being invited, she just kind of moved in. "At first I didn't care," he said, "but, now I feel like I'm being used. And besides I don't have any romantic feelings for her anymore and the only feelings I do have, is the happiness I will feel when she's gone!" He told me that once he got to the apartment he was booting her out.

305

When we got to his apartment he paid me and told me to wait a few minutes. He grabbed his luggage from the trunk and disappeared into the lobby of his apartment building. I sat there for about ten minutes until he emerged from the lobby with his girlfriend in tow. He tossed two garbage bags of her stuff into the trunk and handed me a twenty dollar bill and said take her away. I was shocked by the girl's objections. There weren't any! She appeared perfectly fine as if she was expecting this all along. They exchanged a brief hug and a peck on the cheek. I then drove her to another apartment building in fort Gary where another man met her in the lobby. Mind you, it was a more upgraded building which made me sing the theme song of the television show in '70s, The Jefferson's, 'Moving On Up'. None of my business I thought as I drove away. At least everyone seems to be smiling about it.

Ingrates: Part and Parcel of the Job

*I*t is said that it takes all kinds of people to make up a world but I find ingrates the most annoying. Let me share with you a few examples that cab drivers universally hate.

Number 1: Puking in the back seat of the taxi and not making any effort at cleaning it up, or even offering the driver a few extra bucks for their mess.

Number 2: There are those who call a cab while at the bar, and when the taxi arrives the driver has to go in and remind them many times before they move, talking to everyone and their dog on the way out. This was what I loved about Dorothy because she would roar at the straggler by saying, "Shut your blabbering and get the hell out of here! This poor driver is trying to make a living, he hasn't got time to wait hand and foot on you!

There are a lot of other people who called a cab and he needs to get to them too! Now get going ass wipe! If you miss this ride I will not call you another one!" Only Dorothy could get away with this. If I did this there would be a fight and I would end up without a fare. Instead the guy would instantly and profusely apologize to me and make his way to my taxi and would smoothly hop right in.

Number 3: How about when a driver picks up a fare at a grocery store during a furious rainfall and the young married couple giggles like kids as they scamper into the back seat leaving the two overloaded grocery carts at the curb and expect the driver to get soaked as he loads them into the trunk. To top it off they won't even give the driver a nickel tip for his troubles.

Once, when this happened to me, I didn't move. I stayed behind the wheel indifferent to the carts sitting on the curb soaking up the rain. The gal looked at me disbelievingly and said, "Aren't you going to put my groceries in the trunk? I answered with a snide comment which I rarely do, but because of her ungrateful attitude, my temper got the better of me. I answered with contempt when I said, "Do I look like a servant to you? Then in a more civil voice I said, "I don't mind *helping* you with your groceries but I refuse to be treated like a slave". My comment must have hit home because they hopped out and I helped them load their groceries into the trunk. I did the same when I got them home, though in silence. They were gracious about it because they gave me a five dollar tip. All I wanted was fairness.

Number 4: How about those ingrates who bring their dogs with them with their paws full of sand and mud, and make no effort at restraining them; even as they hop around and try to climb over the seat and lick the driver's neck as he's driving; or how about those pet lovers who bring their cats in those cute little cages meowing non-stop for the entire ride.

<u>**Number 5:**</u> Then there are those who think the driver knows every street, back alley, and lane in the entire city, even those newly constructed suburbs. This was in the days before GPS came along. They implied that I was incompetent because I didn't know where an obscure street or lane may be.

Wisecracker

*Y*ou never know what you're going to hear coming over the radio from one minute after another. Some are quite hilarious.

I remember one dispatcher who never smiled, who was always serious, drivers referred to him as Dead Pan Sam. One morning as he was dispatching, a new driver excitedly tried to report that he spotted someone trying to flag him down at the bus stop on Henderson Highway and Johnson. He couldn't pick the gentleman up because he already had a fare in the car with him at the time. As he drove slowly passed him at the bus stop he quickly managed to roll his window and shout to the potential fare that he would have the dispatcher send him a taxi. With urgency in his voice he began relaying as much information in as quick a time as possible. He began by saying, "there's a 10-8 (street fare) on the corner of Henderson Highway and Johnson. He's wearing a green bomber jacket with a dark stripe running down the sleeves, there's a matching colored number 88 on the chest. He's wearing a black baseball cap with the same number on the cap. Oh, he's carrying a black attaché case and a large black umbrella!" At this point the dispatcher, in exasperation, interrupted the rookie cabbie and gruffly said, "I'm not working with foolscap here you know. Should I send for fingerprints before the driver picks him up?" As is often the case with people who try to flag down a taxi, he jumped into another cab before our driver got there.

Gnome Fights Back

I have seen a lot of odd looking people walking along Main Street in Winnipeg over the years, but every once in a while, I would see someone that would stand out above the dysfunctional crowd. On this one Friday night I spied this weird looking gnome-like character, who intermingled with the crowd all evening long. I observed him stop and talk with various people, then, he would reach into his pocket and pull out a lighter and light someone's cigarette. At other times he would pull out some coins and hand them over to someone who had approached him asking for cash. At other times, I observed him enter, then, later, exit, several bars during the course of the evening. At first I simply dismissed him as a weird, strange, character. Someone, I thought, who had wandered away from their bunk at the group home. Someone who was basking in the chaotic excitement of the carnival-like evening. At Some point, I lost all track of him. It wasn't until long after the bars had closed and after, the last of the bar patrons had managed to flag down a cab and get themselves home. I returned to the area looking for stragglers. To my surprise the man was still here. Now that the streets were deserted, I took my time in assessing this gnome when I spied him but, this time, I took the opportunity to observe him in more detail. He was a few inches above five feet tall. Though it was late fall, it looked like the man was overdressed for the weather, in terms of warmth. He wore a green nylon winter parka, zipped right up to his throat. A fur trimmed hood covered his head with the draw stings done up tightly under his chin. A wide belt, buckled at the waist, which was drawn so tight, that it pinched his slim waist, forcing the material below the belt to flare out, like a skirt. He wore a heavy dark pair of work wool pants, and tan leather hiking boots with heavy wool socks extending over the boots above his ankles. The laces ended and were tied just below the knee. He was indeed, a colorful, odd looking, character.

I was parked just around the corner from Main Street, on Higgins, sipping on a coffee when a man staggered up to him and asked him for some spare change. I was able to witness their exchange and analyze this character objectively, for myself. I noticed that this gnome stood face to face, self assuredly, keeping eye contact with his beggar. The interchange lasted only a few minutes but it gave me the opportunity to hear the conversation and come to my own conclusions. He spoke with sober eloquence as he gladly emptied his pocket of change. I could tell the gnome was sober and in full control of his faculties. When the beggar slipped as he turned to walk away, Mr. Gnome quickly reached out and grabbed him in a bear hug, steadying him until the beggar regained his footing. The gnome walked the stranger over to a nearby bus stop and spoke encouraging words to him until he could maneuver on by himself. I knew that this character was compassionate, intelligent, educated, charitable, and rational. In between each trip I returned to the area to see is he was still around, and sure enough he was. Later, when the buses had stopped running, the bars closed, patrons all gone home, I observed this same gnome character step out of the all night eatery chomping on a hamburger and sipping on a coke. At the time I was parked across the street on Higgins in the old CPR parking lot. Just then a police cruiser came around the corner and pulled up along the sidewalk and stopped next to the munching man. I couldn't hear their conversation but it didn't last long and soon the cruiser moved on. A short time later the same squad car with the same two officers returned, only this time they pulled over to the spot where this guy was still eating leaning up against a building. The conversation continued from where it left off. It looked to me like the officers were trying to be intimidating but the man was having none of that. I pulled up a little closer to hear what was being said. Soon they were arguing, then the cops became confrontational and again the man stood his ground speaking confidently, but respectfully, to the officers. When one of the officers announced that Mr. Gnome was under arrest, he defiantly asked him, under what charge. There was no legitimate reason to arrest him. He hadn't broken any laws and he wasn't causing any trouble. As the parties argued, it became loud which soon attracted a few onlookers, including me.

Suddenly, the younger one of the officers lunged forward and violently grabbed the man by the arm, attempting to push him up against the cruiser. The gnome violently resisted. He aggressively fought back which soon saw, the two officers lying on the sidewalk in pain. In a flash, another cruiser pulled up at the scene and the two officers from that cruiser joined the fracas. As hard as they tried, they collectively couldn't subdue the pedestrian. He was obviously no slouch! A minute later, another cruiser joined the dance and, even with six officers mixed into the fray, they didn't fare any better. I saw the gnome land a number of punishing blows accompanied with a few well placed kicks landing at the soft spots of the officer's groin. I began to doubt that, even though, significantly outnumbered, the cops might not be able to slap the cuffs on him. Soon, another cruiser screeched up to the melee. The eight officers fought tooth and nail to subdue this determined young man. Eventually, they did. The gnome kicked, punched, and scratched his entire way to the waiting cruiser. Before the cops took off with their victim, they observed all the spectators looking on. Most of us had smirks on our faces. A small group of observers who had congregated to watch the scene kind of moved on in different directions, away from the cops. Before the last officer climbed back into his cruiser a loud voice from the crowd was heard to say, "We'll be watching the papers in case this guy needs witnesses." No one could tell who had spoken those words as the crowd quickly dispersed, nor did the cops make any attempt to find out who said them, but I couldn't have said it better myself. I felt that the message was heard loud and clear. Even in the jungle, people recognize that fair play and justice applies for one and all. This man caused no trouble. He knew his rights and he stood up for them. After all, isn't that what everybody expects and every member of society deserve?

Honesty Feels Good

*H*onesty is always the best policy for anyone engaged in any field of employment. One beautiful sunny summer day in early July, I picked up a group of women, all family members, at the Crossroads Shopping Centre. They had started out for an early morning shopping spree and now, decided to go for lunch at the home of the family members they were visiting. These excited tourists had scheduled to take a tour around Lower Fort Gary, later on in the afternoon. There were four of them altogether, and I drove them to their home in Elmwood. After that fare, I ran off four more trips before getting hungry. Since it got slow, like it often does around noon, I decided to run home for lunch. I ate, and then afterward I got back into my car, that was parked in my driveway. I booked in. I waited for my next trip. Since it was a nice day, my wife joined me as I waited for my next trip.

Suddenly the strained voice of the manager came over the radio and asked me if anyone had left a purse in my car. "Not that I am aware of "I responded, "but I will take a look". I remember thinking, I've run off four fares since those tourists from the shopping centre were in my car, I doubted that the purse would still be in the back seat. If the lady left her purse on the floor in the back seat of my car, it was extremely unlikely it would still be there. I looked. Surprisingly, there on the floor, in the back seat was a woman's purse wide open like a hungry mouth agape, facing the ceiling. I reported that it was indeed there. The manager instructed me to bring the purse to the office, which I did. Curiosity had got the better of me when I spied a bulging brown leather wallet exposed at the opening. I pulled out the lady's wallet and counted thirty nine, one hundred dollar bills. I thought "Wow who carries that kind on cash on them and leaves it in a taxi"? I quickly stuffed the money back into the wallet. After replacing everything back into the purse, I drove to the office. When I arrived there, a well dressed, much relieved, lady greeted me at my car. I told her to check her purse to make sure nothing was missing. Amazingly, nothing was missing. I couldn't believe that none of the next passengers said anything about a purse sitting on the back seat floor or even taken anything from the pure. She attempted to give me a financial reward but I refused. I was relieved too, because if her money would have been missing, I would have been the number one prime suspect. I was more than happy to avoid that and I felt good that I didn't try to take advantage of the situation as I know many would have done.

In Need of Rescue

Sometime during the doldrums of winter I was dispatched to pick up a young woman at the Cross Roads Shopping Centre. She was a nice looking woman, but I sensed that there was something off about her, though it took a bit of time to come to any sort of conclusion. She seemed confused as to where she wanted to go. I tried to engage her in conversation so I could evaluate my assessment of her metal condition. She spoke in short choppy sentences much as an elementary kid would talk.

As we drove along, she started to tell me that people who hire women for employment shouldn't demand that they wear very short skirts or low cut blouses. Plus they shouldn't touch them in private places on their bodies. I agreed with her wholeheartedly and told her that if that ever happened to her, it was important for her to get help immediately, either through her boss or the police. She told me that it was her supervisor at the residential home where she lived, who had engaged her in inappropriate sexual touching.

I could tell the lady was mentally challenged and unaware as to what to do. She was as an innocent child and a victim. I explained to her that whatever happened to her, she was not at fault. I told her she needed to put a stop to it now and that once she did, things would get better, but don't wait! As I drove past Canadian Tire on Nairn Avenue, I spotted a police cruiser on the lot. I pulled over and said, "See the police car over there?" She looked at the cruiser on the lot and acknowledged that she saw them. Without wanting to sound too aggressive, I said, "If you want, I can talk to that policeman over there and I can tell them what you told me. I'll tell them you need a little help and I know they will help you." In my most passive voice I asked her permission and waited for an answer. Without hesitation she answered yes. "Good for you," I answered as encouragingly as I could. Then I made my way to the police cruiser and relayed the story to the officers. They listened to me, asked a few questions, and then gently escorted the woman to their car. I stayed where I was, smiling and keeping eye contact with her all the while that I was there. I waved at her when the police car moved away. It was the last time I ever saw her but I had a good feeling about her as she faded down the road.

Weeping and Wailing and Gnashing of Teeth

The title to this little story says it all. This one summer evening I was driving a woman and her six year old son to her uncle's house in the north end. She was comely and looked intelligent. She told me that once she dropped off her young son, she was then going on to the airport to catch a flight for Yellowknife in the Northwest Territories'. She was planning on staying there for a whole year. She had landed a good paying job and was looking forward to saving a lot of money. Everything seemed calm in the taxi as we drove to her uncle's house. When we got there, I pulled over to the curb and they both hopped out of my taxi. With her son in toe, they made their way into the house unimpeded. The mom, her son and his knap sack. I waited at the curb facing the street. After a couple of minutes, mom scooted out the front door with her son right behind her back screaming and raging on like a wild tiger. He kicked, thrashed with every fibres of his being. He broke free but her uncle grabbed the boy and brought him into the house. As soon as he put him down inside the door, the child instantly roared in a fit of crying rage, broke free from his uncle's grasp and made it out to the veranda. The uncle had a very difficult time to overcome the child's incessant tears. It took a long while to get the kid inside the house, but once he did, the child fought like a tiger so violently that the uncle lost control of him again. The kid was wrestling away from his uncle's grip, almost successfully. Finally, the uncle grunted the order to his niece to get in the taxi and go. That's exactly what she did though we couldn't escape the roar of the terrified child's cries piercing the night air. The cries stayed with us until the taxi drove out of range, which was three block away. I had never heard a child in so much distress and emotional pain as that child expressed in his rage. I wiped tears away from my eyes as I drove away. I noticed mom wipe a tear or two away as well. All I could think to tell her was that she had better phone her son once she arrived at her destination and try to ease his pain. The sounds of that child's cries haunted me for a long time afterwards.

All in the Family

I remember one time as the bars were closing, I got a call to pick up a gentleman at the Airport Hotel, way down Ellis Avenue. My passenger turned out to be a well dressed middle aged man. As I was driving him to Elmwood, he told me that he watched his daughter perform her strip tease act that night. That statement utterly shocked me and made me feel uneasy. Although I had no children at the time, I felt sick to my stomach. I just couldn't imagine watching my child, whom I had raised since childhood, and taking delight in watching her strip under any circumstance. He seemed to take an uneasy delight in her sensuous performance.

Many years later I went back to school at University and became a social worker. Now, I can see that such an event indicates sexual abuse just like when a young girl starts to slit her wrists. It screams pedophilia simple and clear! This was the only time I ever met this man but, based on what I know now; this father was probably sexually abusing his daughter at a young age. But don't worry folks; the truth always comes out in the end. Then there's hell to pay!

Turn the Tables

*L*ike I've illustrated throughout this book, getting ripped off or beaten out of a fares occurs almost daily. It feels like a battle of will. This one day early Saturday morning, I picked up an aboriginal man and I drove him to the corner of Inkster and the Perimeter highway. That was way out in the boonies. The fare ran twenty four dollars. That was a big fare back then. He shuffled around through his pockets for money but I could tell he didn't have any. Finally in futility he announced he had no money. He pulled a jack knife out of his pocket and offered it to me as payment. I remembered seeing them on sale for $3.99 at the Army, Navy Surplus Store. I told him to keep the knife and out of frustration I asked him why he would take a taxi that distance only to rob me out of the $24.00 fare which I would be expected to cover by my boss, Chuck. He looked down at the floor and apologized. He said he had been away from his wife and children a long time and he just had to see them again. They lived on reserve in northern Manitoba. I asked him how he was going to get from where we were to where they were with was another four hour drive. He said he was going to hitch-hike the rest of the way. He was under the influence but he wasn't drop dead drunk. His words touched me, being a father and all. We had a long talk about his family and I told him I understood where he was coming from but he had done wrong. After a lengthy talk we shook hands and I wished him the best of luck. I slipped him all the tips I had earned that night which was more than the fare, I was out all that cash but I felt good about it.

7-11 Flunkie

ometime in the 1970s, 7-11 stores were at their height in popularity. So too was the fact that most of them employed East Indian men to work there. That night, though I had worked a long shift, I decided to walk home. The reason being, that the weather was exceptionally mild and I felt energized. It was just a bit over a mile to my home but I figured I could handle it and I could sleep once I got home. There was a 7-11 at Watt Street and Neil and the same gentleman worked the night shift regularly but he developed a bad habit. When he got very sleepy, sometime in the middle of the night, he left the doors to the store wide open. He would then sit in his car facing the wide open doors and sleep soundly.

This particular time, as I approached the store, there he snored behind the wheel of his car. At the same time that I arrived, I spied two men each carrying 2 large paper bags stuffed with items they had stolen. When they saw me, they stopped in their tracks and held their fingers across their lips, nodded their heads to the sleeping man behind the wheel, and continued to tip toe out of the store, only at a faster pace. I couldn't help but laugh at the scene. I made a noise just loud enough to wake the fellow but not scare him and I just continued walking, chuckling under my breath. I wondered how many more folks walked out of that store with bags of free goodies. And, did these two become frequent shopper icons.

Another time when I was in the store, I was making a purchase. As I walked up to the counter and could hear an elevated voice and I watched a man call the clerk a crook because of his high prices for items from the store like snacks and stuff, all the while the price tag of an expensive pair of sun glasses rested of the side of his large nose. The clerk protested in a strained voice and said, "I'm sorry sir, I don't set the prices you know." The customer stormed out of the store leaving his items on the counter but he kept the sunglasses on his face without paying for them. Some people are so crafty and sly.

Wagon Girl

*T*here are days when life feels wonderful and we are moved to deal compassionately with our fellow men. I remember such a day in the summer of 87. It was a Saturday. I had left my home on Clyde Road early, shortly before noon. It was a brilliant, beautiful, bright, sunshiny day. I had finished an early lunch and got a trip taking a couple of shoppers from the Crossroads Shopping Centre to their home somewhere near Concordia Hospital. As I travelled down Panet Road I observed a young girl, who I estimated to be about eleven years old. She was struggling, pulling with great effort, an oversized wagon, overloaded with beer bottles. The rudimentary cart bounced along and I observed the odd bottle drop from the cart with every few half dozen steps. She would stop to pick them up and rearrange the load to accommodate the bottles. It was obvious to me that she was heading to the Gay Cavalier Hotel to cash them in. When I passed her, she was on the east side of the road facing toward the hotel. I slowed when I passed

329

her and it was then that I caught a glimpse of the strain on that little girl's face as she struggled along. It was then that I decide to help her out. I hurried in delivering my passengers to their destination. It didn't take me long and when I caught up to the little wagon girl she hadn't progressed much. At this point her wagon had flipped over, spilling her cargo along the side of the road. She shed a few tears as she silently worked at cleaning up the mess. She was in the process of resettling the bottles onto the cart again when I arrived. I pulled over on the shoulder of the road and stopped in front of her. I was facing the wrong direction so I put on my four way emergency flashers. I greeted her with a smile and asked, "Need a lift sweetie?" She was shy and shook her head no. I told her I could the whole wagon in the trunk. She hesitated but accepted my help. I hustled out of my taxi and put all of the beer bottles in the trunk of my cab. The wagon itself, I managed to load into the back seat along with the extra bottles that we couldn't fit into the trunk. I noticed that one of the wheels was bent a little causing it to rub against the edge as it turned. Eventually, I sped off to the Gay Cavalier Hotel. As we drove to the bar I asked her why she was cashing in her beer bottles. She told me it was her younger brother's birthday that day and her stepdad told the family that he couldn't afford to get the boy a birthday present but her mother promised to bake him a cake. The little girl felt bad for her brother and she didn't want him to go another year without a birthday present. So she adamantly decided to take matters into her own hands and she scoured her entire home and collected every beer bottle she could find on the premises. I hustled around the back to the beer retail outlet and cashed them all in. I poured a pile of cash into the girl's hands afterwards. Then I drove her and the wagon back home. She was very thankful and she waved to me as I drove away. I was touched by her story but I was even more moved when I dropped her off at home. Her home was on Gateway Road at Munroe. That was a long way from where I picked her up. That means she not only spent an hour or two collecting all those bottles from around the house, she also spent more time loading her makeshift wagon. Then she struggled, all by herself, with that wagon with the bent wheel, all the way down Munroe to Panet Road where I happened upon her. She was yet willing to struggle all the way back again, with that wagon. This was indeed a Godly child! I was more than happy that I added my float to the cash I gave her when I handed over the beer bottle sales into her saintly hands. It was my privilege to add my part into it.

Boxed In

I remember one period of time in the 1970's when a native gentleman came to work at Red Patch Taxi. I remember this driver who sounded chronically punch drunk, who always had a wisecrack to say to the dispatcher. It caught my attention because I found him funny. Most of the time I couldn't tell if he really was drunk or just plain goofy. I started paying closer attention. I asked the other drivers what was up with this new guy. I found out that he was the 1951-52 Canadian heavyweight boxing champion. One day as I strolled through the Winnipeg arena, I accidently stumbled over to the makeshift Winnipeg Sports Hall of Fame, which consisted mainly of pictures of Canadian champion athletes. Large pictures of these celebrated athletes hung on the wall and there, I saw Jim, poised in typical intimidating fighter mode.

Communication between driver and dispatcher needs to run smoothly and efficiently. A simple example might go something like this: His driver's number was 22 and when Jim said that number he added extra emphasis to the number 22. Jim spat the two numbers out of his mouth, as if he had gotten a punch in the belly, forcing each number out of his mouth individually. He made it sound guttural and Goofy like. The narrative like this;

Dispatcher: 22
Driver: 2.....2, Portage and Main
Dispatcher: Lasalle Hotel for Peter
Driver: 10...4

It was perfect for Jim to seize this opportunity to demonstrate his uncanny nervy punch drunk alliteration, by sounding-out-each-number-separately in the deepest base voice he could muster. Slow and deliberate in speech. It sounded like he got a powerful punch in the gut and he couldn't catch his breath.

Some times a driver would ask the dispatcher for directions such as, "What's the fastest way to the airport from here?" Jim would quickly grab his microphone and with great enthusiasm and in his deepest, goofiest, voice, would answer, "By car!!" then he would chuckle.

Another time I heard a nervous new driver ask the dispatcher something. (The driver's name was Doug and the dispatchers name was Bobby). It went like this. 47! Go ahead 47! The driver asked nervously, "Did you call me Bobby?" Before the dispatcher could answer, Jim grabbed the mike and said, "No, he called you Doug!" speaking again in his trademark voice and highlighting it with his goofy chuckle. All the drivers laughed at times like that. Everyone enjoyed Jim's humor and they all respected him.

Unfortunately Jim's taxi driving career came to an end one early summer morning. Jim had dropped off a fare at the bus depot and since he didn't need to return to Elmwood just yet, he stayed parked in front of the depot hoping to snag a street fare. At that moment a driver from our competitor, Yellow Cab, pulled up close behind him touching his rear bumper, at the same time, another Yellow cab pulled up in front of him, and backed up until their bumpers touched in front, boxing Jim in. The two Yellow Cab drivers got out of their cars along with Jim and a heated argument ensued. The two Yellow Taxi drivers were attempting to gang up on Jim, thinking they were going to lay a beating on Jim. They stupidly believed that they could spook Jim away from the bus depot. In reality everyone knew there was no concession anywhere on Portage Avenue, including the space in front of the bus depot. Sometimes though, certain drivers from other companies tried to intimidate us away from that location because it could be quite lucrative. Soon, a flurry of punches from Jim resulted in two Yellow Cab drivers with broken jaws knocked unconscious. As a gesture of dignity, Jim picked them up and gently laid them on the hood of their cabs, pulled the front car forward, then drove away.

Believe it or not Jim was charged with assault even though the two younger men tried to assault him, and were the instigators in all of this. The judge said that because Jim was a trained fighter, had assaulted theses two troublemakers with lethal weapons, his fists. Now, because his fists were classed as weapons, he was found guilty and took away his license. It was a cruel and unjustifiable verdict and the law should be ashamed. I see it as just another example of racist mindset toward native people in our country. It was wrong and shameful. Whoever that judge was should be ashamed and perhaps he could have served society if, instead of becoming a judge, sold shoes for a living.

First to Come, First to Go

While that title sounds good, if you're going to a fire sale, it is highly outrageously offensive to the cab driver who is trying to make a living. I'm talking about the self centered, inconsiderate, selfish people who, when they need a cab, call many taxi companies all at once, and whichever cab shows up first, that's the one they leave in. They don't care about the driver's loss in terms of gas, wear and tear on the car, but even more concerning is the loss of the driver's time. The time that that driver spent getting to your door means time lost getting to someone else's door, somebody who really wants a taxi. Now, the other people waiting for a cab must wait even longer. I was shocked and somewhat upset when it first happened to me.

On this particular rare occasion I was working days. It was sometime in mid February. It was a cold sunny mid morning, after rush hour, so it was quiet. I was sent to a home in Transcona. I drove onto the shoveled out driveway and waited a couple of minutes for the woman

336

to come out and get in the back seat of my car. As soon as she closed the door, I put the cab in reverse and backed into the front of another vehicle, which turned out to be a Duffy's taxi. It startled me a little bit because it was unexpected. Being somewhat upset about it, I quickly stepped out of my car and went to confront the Duffy's driver for an explanation. The driver was an elderly man who told me that his company also received a call from this same lady requesting a taxi to take her to the Medical Arts Building on Portage Avenue. The driver told me that this address was known for pulling these kinds of stunts. Still being green in the business, I asked him what we should do. He said that when this sort of thing happens, the two or more drivers who show up usually chat amongst themselves. Then they usually agree to ultimately leave the selfish, inconsiderate people standing in their driveway, and drive away. That sounded like a justifiable plan to me. After I agreed, I opened the back door of my taxi, leaned into the back seat and asked the lady to step out, as we had decided to vacate the fare. She was outraged but not as much as we were. I shook hands with the Duffy's driver and bade her good-by. I waited on a side street for a bit to make sure the other driver did not leave with her, but shortly after he passed my street with an empty car. I was out the trip but boy did that feel good. It felt like there was justice served here.

Personal Weapon Pays Off

*O*f all the bars in the entire city of Winnipeg the very worst one in terms of violence, or crime, was located just off Portage Avenue, on Notre Dame. I don't remember the name of the place any more, but I do remember the cops finally shut it down after being called there relentlessly. There were stabbings, brawls, fist fights, the odd shooting, and hookers hung around the place in hordes, freely plying their trade. As for cabbies, they loved the place! Not necessarily to plot any criminal activity, although, if they wanted to, they could have easily amassed the personnel to accomplish any illegal scheme they could hatch in their brains. The main entrance faced King Street and once you passed through the front doors, a flight of stairs immediately descended down into the busy main bar. Cops referred to the place as the "hell hole". Drivers didn't hang around the place too

338

long, but most made it a priority to pick up the easy fares and take off. Once they left the area, taxi drivers sat near the other bars on Main Street that were less challenging, like the Occidental. On occasion I sat directly across the street from the front doors which gave me a clear viewpoint of the place. If something ever went really bad, as it always did, I could put the cab in gear and take off. Like I said I witnessed many bizarre things at that place, like stabbings and so on. I remember seeing guys stagger out of the bar with a knife sticking out of their chest or a man, once in a while a woman, clutching their chest in their attempt to stop the blood gushing through their fingers, spilling through to the sidewalk.

I remember one late evening as I sat in my cab across the street from that hell hole, in my usual vantage spot, I viewed a very large, burly, bounder, of a guy with a loud mouth step through the main doors with a flashy hooker on each arm. A Duffy's taxi sat directly in front of the doors with a thin jockey size driver behind the wheel. For no reason, this attracted the attention of this bounder. After the 2 hookers got into the back seat he walked around to the driver's window and started giving him a hard time. I was confused as to why he was doing this because, after all, he was hiring the cab to drive him somewhere. This didn't make sense! As near as I could figure, I thought that this loud mouth bully, was simply mean and loved to hurt innocent people. It looked to me like he was intending to lay a beating on this defenseless driver. He loudly intimidated the driver, threatening to pulverize him, cursing and verbally abusing him, as chronic bullies like to do. Finally, the bully opened the driver's door. It swung wide open, exposing the driver to the world. I felt a sickening knot in the pit of my stomach because I thought I was about to see a bloody beating on a person, much smaller than the loud aggressor who was bent on carrying out the crime. The aggressor then slapped the driver across the face and I thought, the beating was starting to happen. It was at this point that things changed dramatically! I had a full uninhibited view of everything going down. When the bully slapped the cabbie, he attempted to deliver it with every ounce of strength he had, suggesting that he wanted to inflict the maximum amount of pain possible. This huge man, in his attempt to deliver the blow, lost his balance, and fell on his butt, so that he landed in a sitting position on the wet, icy street. It was then that I noticed a chrome metal tube attached to the side of the driver's seat protruding up like a western gun holster. In a flash the cabbie sprang out of his taxi grabbing, what looked like, a length of a hockey stick that protruded from the chrome holster. He quickly and aggressively, delivered a savage blow that landed with force, across the aggressor's forearm. How quickly things changed. The loud mouth bully, (are there any other kinds) yelled out in pain. Now it was the taxi driver with an 18 inch long hockey stick who was in charge. In a second the bully went from aggressor to beggar. Now it was the spindly cabbie standing over the kneeling bully who was doing the threatening. The bully, now on his knees, held his hands, fanned out in front of himself pleading for mercy. No longer a bully, now a coward, A real manifestation of his true character. He waved his fingers in front of his face, his fingers spread out like a flimsy fan, his only protection. The driver cursed a few colorful words of his own, and delivered a vicious blow rattling across the ten widely spread fingers, the sounds testifying that many fingers were now broken. The bully never held back on his pain. "Please, please, please, don't hurt me, I'm sorry! I'm sorry!"He pleaded, all the while waving his hands frantically hoping to avoid another blow and kindly obtain mercy. Now, I, was starting to feel sorry for the bully; loud mouthed, or not. The driver yelled that if he ever approached him again he would finish the job. The driver quickly turned and hopped back behind the wheel of his cab and spun away, the hookers still in the back seat. The spectators who had witnessed the show didn't look forward to police interviews, and quickly disappeared back inside the bar. When I drove away, the area looked deserted. All I could see was a sobbing bully covered in blood lying flat out on the street blubbering in pain like a baby. Sometimes, justice is just, though, sometimes cruel.

Roughneck Driver

*I*n my early years of driving cab 1 had amassed a horrendous driving record because 1 was always in a hurry. Lucky for me, 1 never killed myself or anyone else, which 1 believe, that, that in itself, was an accident. Many times on payday 1 barely had enough money left over, after paying all my traffic violations, speed being the most detrimental to me. 1 remember being called in to the license bureau for an interview so they could decide whether they should pull my driver's license or not. 1 nervously drove down Portage Avenue where a stern personnel officer questioned me. 1 told him 1 had undergone serious marital problems which my wife and 1 had resolved through a church official, and now we expected clear sailing. The interviewer looked at me suspiciously, but warned me that if he saw one more infraction appear on my driving record that 1'd be looking for a new line of work. 1 left his office with a great deal of relief. For the longest time 1 avoided any more speeding tickets and accidents but that was only because I was instructed to take a defensive driving course. It helped me a lot. A year or so later the accident and speeding tickets returned. Instead of learning to slow down and avoid accident I learned to hate the cops because I felt they were victimizing me because I was an easy target. It took many more years for me to finally smarten up. But, meanwhile.....................

One windy, cold, sleet filled day, I was driving way up Henderson Highway heading for Lockport. Like usual, I was speeding. My wipers were making a heck of a racket because I had huge chunks of ice frozen to then. The noise was not only deafening, but annoying. I noticed the cop only once I passed his radar trap. This happened just past the perimeter. I was ticked, knowing I was caught, when I flew by. As usual, he sped up behind me and put on his red bubble light as he flashed up behind me. I was seething behind the wheel in my seat as I waited for the officer to approach my window. The sleet continued to pelt my windows and the wind blew hard as I watched the officer gather up his paraphernalia. I was so upset that I considered punching him out. I was weighing out my options if I actually chose this stupid line of action. He gave a sharp rap on my side window. Meanwhile, I had already taken my driver's license, Insurance card, and registration document out, and I had them held in place, pinched by my electric window which now flapped wildly in the wind. Without even looking at him I loudly barked, "Everything's there. Take them and go write your ticket!" I hoped he'd get to feel the full effects of this blustery weather. I prayed the wind would blow his hat off his head and hopefully, land under the wheels of a passing transport. The officer rapped at my window again, but this time, much harder. With a crimson screwed up face, he shouted in my ear, "Do you know you were going sixty miles an hour in a fourty mile an hour zone!?" In an almost equally loud voice I shouted back, "Yes, I know, I had to slow down for the bend in the road!" Immediately, he swung open my door and spoke like a drill sergeant and said, "Follow me, smart ass!" He then took my documents from the window, spun on his heels and headed back to his cruiser. He clipped the paper work to his metal board and I followed him. When we settled ourselves in his car he started harping on me about my driving. I was still seething because I felt victimized by the evil cops who were all out to get me. I knew I was being unreasonable but I was angry. I cut him off as I said, "Just give me the stinking ticket you've been dying all day to give me, and let me go so I can continue to try to make a living and support my family!" The cop tore viciously into me and told me to shut up. Then he proceeded to lecture me for the next twenty minutes, non-stop. The most amazing thing about this whole episode is that he actually never gave me a ticket, which surprised the heck out of me. I did appreciate him giving me a break because I knew that I was in the wrong and it was my responsibility to drive defensively. This lesson stayed with me for a number of years and helped me keep a clean record................

Then one day as I was approaching the airport another cop stopped me for speeding. Again the cop roared in my face that when he saw my vehicle on his radar screen, he said he thought it was a jumbo jet coming in for a landing! Being flippant as usual, I asked, "When did you realize that I wasn't a jumbo jet!" Without missing a beat, he, responded, "Jumbo jets can't travel that fast!"

With that quick retort I knew I was beat, and I gave up. This time I got a speeding ticket. Again for a while I managed to slow down and stay out of trouble but sometimes slow isn't good enough...........One very cold winter January evening, I was slowly driving up Selkirk Avenue. Driving conditions were treacherous that night. The roads were ice covered as I drove in the right lane. There was a vehicle beside me, only he was in the centre lane. We were neck in neck approaching Salter. Suddenly the driver pulled into my lane and when he did, he cut me right off. If he had kept up the speed he did when he pulled in front of me, it would have been okay, but he just took his foot off the gas and slowed right down. I tried to stop but I was skidding, I could not stop. It was evident that I was going to hit him because there was nowhere to safely go. Suddenly I detected a young child's head through the frost covered window. I feared for the safety of the child and immediately swerved to the right and drove into a telephone pole at the curb. The crash screwed up my front end but there was absolutely no damage to the other vehicle. I was glad that I was driving slowly at the time, even better, the child escaped unscathed. I reported the accident to my dispatcher. After we exchanged particulars, a tow truck towed me to the garage. The dispatcher asked me if I wanted to take out another taxi. Without hesitation, I said, "Sure, why not?" Within a short time I was out cruising the streets, looking for street fares. I figured if the company had that much confidence in me, I didn't need to hesitate to continue working. I'm either a good driver or I'm calloused enough to become one, so I stayed on the road.

I would wager that virtually all taxi drivers anywhere in the world have horrendous driving records. That's mostly because cab drivers drive over a hundred thousand miles (not kilometers) a year, then add the fact that cabbies drive twelve hour days into the mix. Also, they drive under extreme driving conditions like ice storms, blizzards, torrential rains, sleet; hail and anything else nature can throw at them. One of the things about Manitoba weather is this. You can go to work under a sunny sky and as you move along throughout the day, the temperature drops dramatically. But, you're in a nice dry warm car, so you don't notice that the streets are slicker than the Winnipeg Jets hockey arena. You drive along down a street where the road makes a sharp bend. You frantically turn the wheel in the direction you want to go but the car says, up yours, as you plow straight ahead into an oncoming vehicle. Like a Toyota commercial, I repeat, Oh! What a feeling! I have experienced those Toyota feeling more than once. It's not a time for a Kodak moment.

Pick a Lane!

*A*fter driving taxi for twelve years I arrogantly came to see myself as an above average driver, superior over everyone else in the fleet. This, despite the fact that I had many speeding tickets and a few accidents to my credit. It had been a long while since any new infractions had occurred so you could say I forgot my past driving record. One Thursday after noon I was leaving Transcona via the highway at rush hour. I was heading west into Elmwood. The traffic heading east into Transcona was thick when I noticed a transit bus stopped at the rail tracks. I paid no notice of this as I was used to seeing buses stopped at rail crossing. However, what I didn't look for was the traffic flowing into Transcona behind the bus. Immediately, having passed the bus, an oncoming vehicle was driving too quickly to avoid crashing into the rear of the bus, heavily loaded with passengers. The middle aged woman, who was driving the Cadillac, was on her way home from work and became distracted for a second. She did not realize the bus was approaching the tracks and that by law they were required to stop. She instantly realized that she was not going to be able to avoid a collision with the bus. Without touching her brakes (I know this because her vehicle didn't skid to a stop) she simply swerved around the bus and drove head on into my taxi. The traffic was moving along pretty steady at the time so we were probably moving at eighty Kilometers an hour. When she connected with my vehicle it pushed me into the car beside me as well as causing a number of cars behind me to crash into each other forming a pile up. Miraculously, I sustained no injuries however; the car was a write off. The car of lady who caused the accident required towing and she needed an ambulance. She was later charged with careless driving. I was mostly angry at this accident and I was going to quit driving cab altogether. The manager took me into his office and convinced me that this accident was not my fault and I needed to take a day off and come back so as not to lose confidence in myself. I took his words to heart and continued driving for many more years!

Today when I see people driving half in one lane and half in another I usually roll down my window and shout as loud as I can, "Pick a lane! Any lane! Jerk!"

Shoulda Ducked!

*B*eing a career taxi driver means you're moving around the city and beyond, at least twelve to sixteen hours a day, six day a week. It means that over time, you happen upon events and spectacles that leave an indelible mark in your memory. It really has nothing to do with driving a taxi other than being there to witness some jaw dropping events. Here is one of the most glaring ones.

This one happened one weekday, on a lazy, summer morning, an hour or so after the early morning rush, when the day was grinding into its busy routine. I was returning from dropping off a senior citizen at the Medical Arts Building on Portage Avenue. I had just picked up some breakfast and I was going to park by the river and eat it. I drove over the first hump of the Disraeli Freeway and I took the exit ramp right onto Talbot Avenue. I drove to Brazier then turned onto Midwinter. I had a perfect view of the Red River. I spotted a window delivery truck driving towards me laden down on both sides of the box with the maximum amount of commercial glass windows, to the point that it was obvious to me that it was loaded to maximum capacity. As a matter of fact, I believed it was over maximum capacity. Some of the glass windows had to be twelve feet in height. Suddenly as the driver attempted to drive underneath the overpass, not realizing that the distance from the road to the overpass was lower than the top of his cargo, came to a dead stop about half way to the back of his truck. Glass exploded in every direction. Instantly the delivery truck got wedged in underneath the overpass. It was as far as the driver was able to go. I don't know how fast the driver was moving, but I don't think he was speeding. Mind you, he didn't have to be speeding to cause the damage he caused. I gasped at the sight and just held my breath for a few minutes. As I pulled forward to see if the driver was all right the driver emerged from the truck. It didn't take me long to conclude that every single pane of glass on that truck was broken; every window of every size and dimension that he carried on both sides of his truck were DESTROYED! Every sheet of window was now destined for the landfill site. "You okay?" I hollered. The river emerged from the truck and stood and looked around at the carnage of glass and just shook his head. I didn't know what to say to ease his discomfort. The old man who was driving this vehicle leaned into the truck and radioed to the shop about the accident, and looked forlorn as he took refuge in a cigarette while he waited for his boss to show up. Really, I thought to myself, he looks like he's waiting for the executioner to show up so he can ream him out good and then, fire him on the spot. I felt sorry for him. The look on his face said he knew he was done. It also said that he knew what results were coming and that he accepted it because there was nothing else to do. I didn't want to stay and stare at the driver and add to his humiliation. I drove off, passing by him on the other side of the road where I stopped. I and quietly said with as much compassion as I could muster, "I might have done the same thing because the height at this point in the road can be deceiving." He made no reply, just took a drag on his cigarette. I added "I'm sure the insurance will cover the damage so your boss's loss won't be too great. He'll get paid for this mess." The driver looked like he was ready to shed tears so I decided to slowly drive away. "My boss won't care, he'll fire me for sure," he said as I drove off. "Hell of a day to begin retirement!" were the last words that I heard him speak. My heart just went out to the driver.

Cops versus Thugs

I've seen a lot of mean, tough looking characters outside the bars of Winnipeg over the years and I always wondered how some fresh rookie cops, still wet behind the ears so to speak, might react when confronted with these mean, rough looking characters. Well, one day I got to witness such an encounter. One Saturday morning, I was parked outside a usually rowdy bar, just off Portage Avenue on Notre Dame. It was shortly before noon, as best as I could tell, since the bar wasn't open yet. Two young beat cops were standing guard over two really rough looking characters. They were standing with their backs to the main door which happened to be made of thick heavy oak. I guessed that they were waiting for the paddy wagon to arrive so that the two thugs could be transferred to jail. The two cops who were probably in their early twenties, looked nervous. Meanwhile the punks looked cocky, menacing, I would even say intimidating. The bigger one wore a black leather jacket and sported a Mohawk haircut. He was the most vocal, cursing at the cops and calling them derogatory names. The other punk was too busy laughing to be a threat. The two men stood with their backs to the locked, heavy, wooden doors. The cops stood facing them, blocking them in case they attempted to get away. It was obvious that the punks were under the influence. Both policemen held one of those very long flashlights, the ones that held multiple batteries. They held them as if they were night sticks. Neither cop spoke; they just tried to look in control.

All of a sudden, the punk with the Mohawk and black leather jacket threw an overhead punch knocking the flashlight out the hands of one of the cops, sending it crashing to the sidewalk. My first thought was, "Oh oh, those cops are in for a beating!" I couldn't have been more wrong. The cop's reaction was instant. He grabbed the punk by the throat and pushed him full force, backwards, sending him crashing into the heavy wooden doors. I heard a loud sickening thud as his head met the wood. I could tell Mr. Mohawk was instantly unconscious. He slithered down the wooden door, leaving a heavy red streak of blood in his wake. In one motion the cop flipped the body over onto his stomach and, faster than a cowboy at the Calgary Stampede, he slipped the cuffs on him while his partner had his long flashlight pressed with force across the other punk's throat. I heard the cop warn his prisoner with, "Move one inch and I will beat you with this flashlight, non-stop, until the paddy wagon comes along. The punk tried to move and the cop then pulled the thug away from the doors a couple of steps, stopped, spun him around so that he faced the doors, then with all the force and strength he could muster, he ran the punk headlong into wooden wall. He too crashed with a thud, and then toppled down to the cement. Instantly the cop straddled his back and slipped the cuffs on his prisoner. In a short time things came to a standstill. Soon, the paddy wagon came along to pick up the trash.

I could see the cops had been nervous dealing with these two over confident creeps but they handled themselves professionally. I felt happy for their excellent training and well deserved victory.

Misplaced Loyalty

*A*s a driver I was amazed when I witnessed one's dire living circumstances. I was even more amazed when I witnessed how a third party attempted to provide aid to that person to the detriment of his own marriage. It wasn't until I drove this older gentleman home several times before I caught on as to what was actually going down.

On this certain Friday night, the dispatcher sent me to pick up this older man at the King's Hotel on Higgins Avenue. It was about ten o'clock at night when I picked him up. When he got into the taxi I could tell he was drunk, as he was all the other times I drove him home. Like usual, he asked me to stop at a certain younger lady's home at some low rental complex. Like usual I waited while he went inside to, as he said, *drop something off for a friend.* I figured the guy was a disgusting skunk. This time the gentleman left the front door to his lady friend's house wide open so that I could see full well what was going on with the woman and her daughter.

Even though I had driven him here several times before, this time I learned firsthand that it was not a man taking advantage of or messing with a younger woman who was financially disadvantaged, It was more like watching the interactions going on between a father and a daughter. For the first time, I saw him reach into his pocket and pull out a roll of bills, the remains of his pay cheque I guessed and place it in her hands. He kept just a couple bills for himself. She was instantly moved to tears. In a tearful voice she said. "You are so kind, helping me out at a time like this when I needed help the most!" Then she threw her arms around his neck and gave him a heart filled hug. He simply patted her on the back tut tutting her like a father consoling a child. I guessed the lady to be in her early thirties, her daughter about 8 years old and he in his early sixties. After a few minutes he broke away from her embrace and came out to his waiting taxi. Once inside he closed the door and I continued on in silence to his home. I still hadn't caught on to the full extent of this man's charity. When I dropped him off at his front door his wife met him outside. After a few words between them she verbally attacked him with derision and rage. She was crying out loud when she said "You drank your whole pay-cheque away, again," she lamented. Through her tears she let out a litany of abuse and derogatory terms before she turned and marched back in through her doorway. The gentleman didn't speak a word but shuffled in behind her like a child rebuked. I was stunned by the event that unfolded before my eyes that night.

Like I said earlier, there was no funny business going on between this older gentleman and his younger, woman friend. He had no ulterior motive in helping her. He did this the only way he knew how and he knew what price he had to pay for doing so. Certainly it was a classic example of misplaced loyalty, dysfunctional as it was.

Deadly Chase

*O*f all the things that I've seen or witnessed, in all my years spent driving taxi, I am surprised that this next spectacle, was seen only once. In the wee hours of a mid-winter Saturday, I was driving down McGregor after having dropped off my last fair on Inkster. I was approaching Selkirk Avenue when a car from my left, travelling approximately 60 miles an hour, flew out of the laneway that ran parallel from Selkirk Avenue. I slammed on my brakes. Hot on the heels of that speeding car came a cop car with the red roof light flashing, keeping up in pursuit. I knew that if I were half a block closer to Selkirk I would have been t-boned and probably killed. I thought that that was ridiculously dangerous of the cops to give such chase. I couldn't understand the rational of them endangering the lives of the public, the occupants of the speeding car, or the officers in the cruiser. I could not be convinced that, even in the case of murder, nothing could justify such reckless mayhem.

Being young and stupid, my next reaction was that this was thrilling. So, I turned right on Selkirk and floored it trying to catch up to the action. Soon, I caught up close enough that I could see the high speed chase taking place which caused me to speed up some more, but when I did, I heard gunshots. The cops were shooting repeatedly at the car they were chasing. Now, if the cops were shooting him maybe he had someone who would be shooting at them! That was when I stopped following the deadly caravan. I chastised myself for being stupid and conclude that since I was functioning at such a dysfunctional capacity, it was time to go home!

Rough Policing

*I*n my capacity as a taxi driver, I saw firsthand, at times, how difficult it could be for Winnipeg's finest as they risk life and limb protecting us. I remember a scruffy young man taunting a police officer, addressing him as piggy. That seems to have been a popular term many punks hurled at cops in the 70's. I remember hearing of a trial in the states where a young punk was charged with calling this police officer: pig! The judge, in this trial, handed down a most appropriate sentence. The defendant was sentenced to join the pigs in a slimy pig pen and wallow in the pig poop with the pigs, until he could tell the difference between a police officer and the real barn yard pigs. I can only imagine it must have been a most humiliating experience.

I know that many cops, while performing their daily duties, get attacked, stabbed and sometimes murdered just doing their jobs. I find it hypocritical when I see large proportions of young people express disdain for cops but it's the cops they run to first when someone steals or damages their property, assaults or harms them or their family members.

When I first arrived in Winnipeg and worked for CN Rail I heard stories from the crew I worked with, about cops being attacked, especially in their rookie years. It sounded like a rite of passage. You're not really a fully fledged police officer, until you've been attacked and beaten by a gang of thugs most probably while patrolling Main Street.

I have witnessed this on occasion, so I know that there is some truth to this tale. Theirs is not a job that I envy. The next tale was told to me by a fare I had from the Transcona police station one summer night.

This one evening around eleven o'clock, I was sent to the police station in Transcona to pick up a gentleman and drive him to his home in North Kildonan. When the gentleman got into my cab he seemed shaken about something, as if he had experienced some trauma. He said nothing for the first little while and then he calmly told me that he had seen the cops enter the cell next to the cell he had been held in that evening, and lay a deadly beating on some transient fellow, for what seemed no reason that he could tell at first. My fare didn't tell me why he was in jail in the first place and I didn't ask. He spoke in hushed tones expressing shock at what he'd seen. "They beat that poor guy almost to death!" he said incredulously. "I never knew cops did things like that!" he whispered as if in fear. Then he said "Suddenly they explained why they were going to mete out vigilante justice on this character."

They said that they knew that he was a child molester recently released from some prison in Ontario. They told him that they had read the disgusting details of his violent crime against an innocent four year old girl. Apparently he had arrived by rail and was living with who knows who doing who knows what, and the cops told him he wasn't welcomed in Winnipeg. If he wanted to live he had better move on: Now!. My fare told me that the officer explained very clearly to the pedophile, what they were about to do to him.

"We don't want you anywhere near our city. In case you don't understand we are going to lay a good beating on you. Then we are going to drop you off at the perimeter highway and when you regain consciousness, stick out your thumb and get away as fast as you can. If you happen to end up in our jail cell tomorrow, the morgue will be your next address! Any questions?" he asked. Before the guy could answer one of the cops whacked him across the shins with a night stick hardy blow. The pervert let out a violent scream in agony. That sound was soon muffled by the many volleys of punches and kicks administered by the group of cops and continued until there was no more sounds escaping the man's lips. When the officers exited the cell the man lay in a crumpled heap on the cement floor. The cretin had lost all his bodily functioning, having peed, puked etc.

Eventually, the officers returned and dragged the man out of the cell just like they said they were going to do and drive him out to the Trans Canada Highway. He said "I can't blame them for not wanting a man like this in their town, especially if they had their own children. It's too bad I had to witness this spectacle because it really shook me up and unnerved me. I don't know what they said to him when they dropped him off but, whatever they told him, I'm sure he wasn't going to come back the next day to ask for clarification. I'd say he got the message!"

A Mother's Pain

I remember on a less violent, but more sombre emotional note, 1 was sent to that same police station in Transcona, to pick up a grieving mother, whose son had gotten himself arrested and imprisoned for drug possession. The kid was just 14 and mom was beside herself with sorrow and self blame. The more she cried the more stumped 1 was as to what to say to help ease her pain and suffering. Sure 1 could quote all kinds of lovely sounding platitudes but 1 doubted it would have helped her. Like most people, they only seek divine guidance when disaster strikes. My wise bishop use to say to our congregation, "Don't wait until you're thirsty before you decide to dig a well. Make Christ your personal friend and learn of Him daily, and practice doing good works every day." That sounded like good advice to pass along to this mother but 1 feared that she might take this to be sounding like blame. 1 know it sounded like that, but 1 have learned a long time ago, that God is the only answer any of us have to guide us through this world. Unfortunately, too many of us wait until we are dying of thirst before we decide to dig that well, and then, the task seems too overwhelming. I always heard my mother telling me that religion is not an organization or some kind of biblical group. Religion is a way of life that must become internalized in our very spirit and used for good toward everyone; and not used for the purpose of Lording over our brothers and sisters. I told this to the grieving mother and urged her to begin on the path of spirituality through reaching out to our Heavenly Father. Prayer would be a great place to start. I asked her if she would like pray right now in my taxi. "I don't know how to pray." She said seeming embarrassed about it all. I haven't prayed since I was a young girl, she stammered.

"Well," I said sounding excited. "Just think how excited God will feel when he hears your voice, calling for His help! Just talk to Him like you would talk to an old friend whom you haven't seen for a long time. Use your thoughts as they come to you." With that, I bore her my personal testimony. With some hesitation she eventually agreed. I then pulled over on the side of the road on that dark night and she prayed. It was from her swollen heart. It was the most beautiful heartfelt prayed I had ever heard. We both wiped away our tears after and I soon drove quietly away. After a long while, that is, just before we got to her home, she asked, "Do you think God heard me?" I sniffed away a sob and answered, "I know

He heard you! Look at us now both crying like two big babies and listen how quiet the world is around us at this moment. The Holy Spirit has testified to our souls that He heard us. Pass that love along to your son every day from now on, no matter what!" I then gave her the name and the address and times of what I believed to be a good bible based church. She wiped her tears and kissed me on the cheek as she got out. I don't know if she followed through on what we talked about after she got home. I only did what I could do, what any of us can do, and that is, I prayed to God to help her get through this. It was an awesome experience for me and I hope, a new beginning for her.

Cops Cool Wild Rider

*D*id you ever find yourself driving along somewhere and all of a sudden, some jerk recklessly flies past you at breakneck speed while cutting in and out of traffic. And you shudder and think to yourself, "Where are the cops when you need them?" You probably wished that you were a cop at that moment and imagined what you would do. I have seen maniacal drivers almost every day that I drove a taxi. I could see myself with my red flashers looming closely behind them. Then once they had pulled over, I would reach across the drivers lap and violently yank the keys out of the ignition and throw them on top of the nearest building or down the nearest drain. Then after I had the driver in cuffs and transported to jail I would wave as the tow truck got hauled away. Tough talk?, Ya, I know but I realize it's only a fantasy of mine that will never happen. However, what I delightfully witnessed one Friday evening came very close to reality that I savored for years.

It happened one Friday evening in late June as I was driving up Notre Dame from Portage Avenue. It was a beautiful evening and traffic was heavy and festive at the same time. Suddenly A 1941 Mercury Monarch convertible zoomed past me driving in the manner I just described only the music coming from its speakers was deafening. The driver had a chick hanging on his arm while another pair sat in the back seat. They were thoroughly enjoying the evening as they sang with the radio and hand dancing as they went along. The sight of it enraged me. My long time fantasy kicked in. I expected that vision would not last long when what to my wondrous eyes did appear an unmarked cop car with two detectives inside were racing after this jerk with their red roof lights flashing. They soon caught up to the jerk with the fast car and the loud music and I soon caught up to them after that. I was filled with joy as I passed them, glad that the vehicle was a convertible because when I passed them I was able to shout loudly with glee, Good! Good! Good! Good! Good!, savoring every word; glad that they could hear it plainly. I think the part I liked best was when I saw the detective reach across the driver's lap and pull the keys from the ignition. I wished that I could have stopped and watched the rest unfold but I think just seeing them pulled over was enough to fulfill my fantasy.

A word on Uber

I wanted to use the final chapter of my book to express my opinions and thoughts concerning Uber. Again these are my thoughts as I see and understand them to be, and it's okay if you don't agree.

I always ask myself how this mega corporation has managed to invade the taxi industry with wanton disregard to the long entrenched rules and regulations that have always existed in the taxi industry. I understand that Uber is worth around 80 billion dollars, give or take a few billion. With that much wealth at their disposal they can do just about anything they want. With that said, I ask myself, did they bribe politicians or other government officials to just sweep those rules and regulations aside and accommodate Uber to step to the front of the line, so to speak. Kind of what one would do when shoeing away a pesky mosquito.

In my experience as a cab driver in Winnipeg, in my day, I know that in order to get a taxi license there were a number of hoops I had to jump through to make that happen. I became aware of the Winnipeg Taxi cab board who had stringent conditions all aspiring cabbies had to follow or else.

I am told that today, if you want to buy a plate (taxi license) in Winnipeg, you can expect to pay well over one hundred thousand dollars, in spite of what the taxi cab board may say otherwise. I have always known that while it was true that the taxi cab board sets the price for the plate, you can expect to pay much more than that when purchasing that plate from a private owner.

In either case, Uber or taxi, you must have a clean driving record. You must submit to a criminal background check. In my day you also had to have a health examination from a local physician. Finally, you had to appear before a panel of senior police officers where you were reviewed about anything on your record and grilled. Also, you were grilled about your knowledge of the city, particularly, where all the hospitals were located. If you have any criminal convictions, don't even bother showing up, look for another line of work.

With Uber, all you need to do is show up with a police criminal background check and fill out an application. You can walk in and walk out in a matter of an hour or two and you're in business.

Herein lays the injustice and controversy surrounding Uber, as I understand it to be. Picture this scenario if you will. You jump through all the necessary hoops to get a taxi license to work six days a week for thirty, forty, or fifty years and retire thinking that you can sell you taxi plate to whoever for a hundred grand or two and enjoy life, right? <u>WRONG!!</u> You put your plate up for sale but the people who show up to purchase your plate choke at the price you're asking for it. Why should they pay you a hundred plus grand for your plate when you can drive for Uber, FOR FREE!!! All you need is to own your own vehicle. You don't need to appear before any taxi cab board, ever! So that poor old schmuck who labored for most of his working life behind the wheel is SCREWED!! And why?, Because Uber is not a taxi, it's a ride share program, a loop hole some lawyer came up with to ruin the entire industry and screw a million or so real taxi drivers out of a lifetime of stressful labour.

Now, I do have to say that as far as the public is concerned riding with Uber is cheaper. Why you ask? Because the Uber Corporation pays the driver a percentage of the trip, then the driver has to cover the hst of the trip plus the gas plus the wear and tear of the vehicle; so who gets screwed in my opinion? The Uber driver! Plus, remember Uber has a much lower operating expense. How can that be you should ask? Think about it. If you owned Uber, you don't need to buy a vehicle! The driver does! But I understand Uber will help with the financing of that vehicle. I don't know that for certain but I did hear of that as a rumour. The part that annoys me the most is the public's perception of Uber. They seem to perceive Uber as trendy. In other words they're snobs and it seems that thought has been infused into society. This is why, you see in movies or in some books the author, for example, will write, *"the killer rearranged the room before he ran out of the apartment and called an Uber to get home"* it sounds trendier to say Uber rather than to say he or she called a cab. Along the same lines you'll hear an actor recite similar lines, giving the scene a trendier aura. Most of the drivers I met never drove a taxi before in their lives which explain why they don't see why they are getting shafted, in that they earn a lot less money. They would have earned much more driving regular taxi. But hey, in this case ignorance is truly bliss!

As for my opinion, I feel Uber should be booted out of the country and the politicians or other government officials who accommodate Uber should be vigorously questioned!

About the Author

*E*mile Proulx was born in Kirkland Lake, Ontario. He graduated from the local high school in 1966, and a few months later he moved to the city of Winnipeg where he gained employment with Canadian National Railway. Fascinated by the functioning and interpersonal dynamics of a wide cross-section of people, he was drawn into the taxi industry. He drove taxi for Red Patch Taxi and stayed employed there for approximately twenty years.

Emile had his first taste of post-secondary education when he attended the University of Manitoba in the '60s taking Arts courses, and later in life obtained a college diploma in Social Work from Northern College in Timmins in 1988, a place he lived in for seven years. Emile is happily married to a native of Winnipeg, a stunningly beautiful girl, Patricia Marceniuk, from Elmwood. Emile is blessed with three wonderful God-given children: Jason, the eldest; Shayne, the teaser; and finally, the long-awaited daughter, Sarah (Pilon) the brat. Emile now resides in Keswick, Ontario, and drives Taxi for Georgina Taxi to supplement his old-age income and as a way to continue to meet and talk with people from all walks of life. This is Emile's first book, but he hopes not his last.

Attention Readers

*F*irst of all, I want to thank you for buying this book. I hope it has brought you some degree of pleasure as you read it. I highly favor your comments because your comments will help me improve as a writer; Be sure to know that I am not fishing for compliments, though I do love compliments, I try to keep my vanity in check. Vanity can only destroy an artist and his work and I think that can also short change you, the reader, which is unforgivable. This book is my first attempt to realize my life-long dream. I have many novels, yet to be born, that have been dancing around inside my head for most of my life. I do not suffer with writer's block, only from lack of confidence, which I believe, I can overcome, when this work becomes popular and succeeds. I want to amass my reader base so that I can email you, the readers, when new novels come out. Consequently, I will be able to bring my latest works to your attention at that time. Thank you Winnipeg! Never have I lived in a more loving place with down to earth people with kind and generous hearts! Thanks again for being you!

Sincerely: E. Eddy Proulx

Please communicate with me via my email which is as follows:

e_eddyproulx@live.ca